Potato Chip Economics:

Everything you need to know
about business clearly and
concisely explained

Potato Chip Economics:

Everything you need to know
about business clearly and
concisely explained

Philip Theibert
and Elizabeth Theibert

**BUSINESS
BOOKS**

Winchester, UK
Washington, USA

First published by Business Books, 2013
Business Books is an imprint of John Hunt Publishing Ltd., Laurel House, Station Approach,
Alresford, Hants, SO24 9JH, UK
office1@jhpbooks.net
www.johnhuntpublishing.com

For distributor details and how to order please visit the 'Ordering' section on our website.

Text copyright: Philip Theibert and Elizabeth Theibert 2012

ISBN: 978 1 78279 034 1

A CIP catalogue record for this book is available from the British Library.

Design: Stuart Davies

Printed and bound by CPI Group (UK) Ltd, Croydon, CR0 4YY

We operate a distinctive and ethical publishing philosophy in all
areas of our business, from our global network of authors to
production and worldwide distribution.

CONTENTS

Introduction   1

Lesson One: The World of Chips – Buying raw materials, making chips, transporting the chips, marketing the chips...   7

Chapter 1. The Real World of Raw Materials or "You can't cook a thought."   8

Chapter 2. Understand the complexity of production: Why you need to know science   37

Chapter 3. Seasoning – and so MUCH more   54

Chapter 4. Packaging   65

Chapter 5. Transportation: Just throw it in the truck. Hmm – bad idea   81

Chapter 6. Marketing Concepts: You Do It So Well   89

Lesson Two: We're from the government and we're here to help you   **111**

Chapter 7. Logic Flies Out of The Window   112

Chapter 8. Unintended Consequences are Expensive   120

Chapter 9. Flexibilty Saves the Day   124

Chapter 10. Ethanol Realities   134

Chapter 11. What is Lobbying and Why Do I Need
to Know About It?   136

**Lesson Three: Some Basic Economics and Administrative
Stuff You Need To Know**   **153**

Chapter 12. Thinking like an accountant   154

Lesson Four: Neat Financial Terms   **173**

Chapter 13. It's More than a Bag of Chips. It's Stocks and
Bonds and Capital Expenditures and Inelastic and
Demand and Other Neat Financial Terms.
Plus LIBOR!!!   174

Chapter 14. Terms Necessary to Understanding the World
of Economics   180

Chapter 15. Multiplier Effect   200

**Lesson Five: Balance Sheets, Income Statements,
Cash Flow – Oh My!**   **207**

Chapter 16. The Balance Sheet Explained   208

Chapter 17. The Income Statement   220

Chapter 18. The Statement of Cash Flows   228

**Lesson Six: Company Cultures – Or why Golden Flake
takes care of its employees**   **233**

Chapter 19. Creating a Positive Company Culture   234

Lesson Seven: How to succeed in business   **247**

Chapter 20. How To Get Promoted   248

Chapter 21. The Players   262

To Richard and Anne, Chiefs of The Birminghams

Introduction

Why this book? Because when I landed my first job in business, I had no idea how business really worked. I was an English major and could not even read a balance sheet, an annual report, had no idea what ROI (Return On Investment) and other esoteric terms (at least to me) meant. And as a public relations consultant, working with a variety of clients, I was close to useless if I did not know the basic elements of business. This 'need to know' what really made business tick intensified when I became a corporate speechwriter and had to talk to shareholders on their terms, in their language. Annual meeting speeches were at first torture to write, but as I became more familiar with those strange business terms, annual meeting speeches were much easier to write.

This book also takes you beyond the nonsense they teach you in Economics 101 and 102, the basic economics courses that even liberal arts majors, despite their best attempts, cannot avoid. So most liberal arts majors escape the university's economics department with a sigh of relief and a very dismal scattering of economic folklore rattling around in their brain.

For instance, how often have you heard the rant, "Economics is based on supply and demand"? Actually that is wrong. This book explores why that concept is wrong by discussing lobbying, competition and how to run a company in survival mode when the big boys are trying to move in on your territory.

A strange segue here. The only way to learn to hit a baseball is to go out and hit a baseball. So this book is not based on lectures or obscure wisdom found in economics departments. This book is based on the real world of business. And to achieve that, I met with the leading executives of Golden Flake Potato Chips, a small Southern-based, successful potato chip company in Birmingham, Alabama. They showed me how business really worked, the real issues they faced every day.

Consider the following two quotes. They exemplify why this book was written, and represent the philosophy behind this book. This book is based on reality, not economic fantasies. Here are the two quotes; both are from Wayne Pate, the former CEO of Golden Flake and now a Director of Golden Flake. As you read the first, I hope you are amazed how much business sense is packed into one quote:

But the sewer, the trucks, the production machines, the storage, the right potatoes – all of that is part of the business of making it work. You gotta be in the marketing business, the commodity buying business, you have to have good relations with your employees, you have to know about vegetable oil, when not to buy it, when you have to buy raw corn for corn meal. Timing is critical in all these things, but assurance of supply is necessary. You cannot gamble if you are going to run a business, you can't cook a thought.

You have to have a product so you have to buy all these things, at prices that you can make work to deliver a finished product that you can sell.

You can't change that wholesale price every day. Consumers, if every time they went to buy chips, the price had changed, they wouldn't be very happy about it. So your prices have to be very stable. So you have to make all the other things work to get to the retail price so your consumers are satisfied.

Another thing that makes a small company survive is always be quality conscious, so no customer will be disappointed when they buy your product. Customers must know that every time they buy our chips, the chips will be good, just like Golden Flake always guarantees.

We want to develop a core of clients that will always buy Golden Flake chips, regardless of what the price is, because they can trust us. And we have learned that promoting it, discounting it, offering "buy one, get one free" does not guarantee steady customers. That just attracts the people looking for bargains, not quality.

And if you get into the game "Who can sell the chips cheaper", the big boys like Frito-Lay will beat you every time. So we will make our chips taste good every time, so customers will say, "Yeah that one is cheaper, but I know that Golden Flake is good and I am going to buy Golden Flake."

That is the importance of "A brand name you can trust."

– Wayne Pate, Director Golden Flake chips

See how much business knowledge was packed into the above quote? Now the following quote emphasizes the knowledge that most economics books don't give you, how the real world works. I know, I know – ironically the quote talks about books.

The real world is not found exactly in a book because a book can only give a certain amount of basic information. And it may be on target – but there are so many things that happen in day-to-day life that you can't put in a book.

One time, the graduate school of engineering at Auburn University wanted to do an energy audit of our plant. We were glad to have them. We work with universities any way we can. We work with Alabama, Samford, Auburn...

So the young man from the graduate school came down off the roof of the plant. He was hot. It must have been 110 in the shade. On that roof it had to be unbearable. He came down and it looked like he had been in a fight.

And his comment was this, "The real world sure is different than being in a classroom. My textbook, those numbers, that table of information I needed was so clear and easy to read. I have to crawl over heater ducts and crack my head on some pipes to get some basic information."

I thought, that is a little thing but that's the way the world

3

really is.

– Wayne Pate

Again, why start off with those two quotes?

Again, they exemplify what this book is about. It is about the complexities of economics, about the real world of business where few things are as easy as they seem.

You just don't pick up a bag of potato chips off the shelf.

The company making that bag of chips, in this case Golden Flake, had to undergo an amazing number of steps, fight an amazing amount of factors, including environmental, regulatory, and financial, just to get those chips to the store.

And that is why this book is important: it will introduce you to the real world of economics. The world they don't teach you in college; it will teach you how business really works, the important things about business you need to know to get and advance in any job.

It will teach you skills you need in the workplace.

Once again, I know these skills are needed because I was an English major and, about six years out of college, through blind luck, landed a job as a corporate speechwriter and I was amazed at how many levels CEOs had to work on. They had to work with legislatures, lobbyists, regulatory agencies, environmental groups, customers, consumers, national, state and local governments, local communities, shareholders, bondholders, investors, banks.

And as a novice corporate speechwriter, I wished I had this book.

A book that taught me the basics of reading a financial statement, what stockholders were, how regulations hampered business, how you marketed and sold a product, how important raw materials were, how you even manufactured a product, how you lobbied for laws in your favor, how you adjusted and readjusted because you had to sell chips at $2 a bag and every time the government raised taxes, or the price of potatoes went up, you had to adjust and readjust.

This book is designed to show you how the economy really works. How supply and demand sometimes have nothing at all to do with setting prices. How one government decision can cause a shortage of raw materials. What your boss or your CEO is really dealing with on so many levels.

And above all, this book is designed to help you get and keep a job. It will help you, when you go into any job interview, to come across as a bright person, who understands the complexities of business, someone who can read a basic balance sheet, yet on a higher level can discuss the current regulations and legislation pending that can hurt your industry.

In short, do you really understand the economy and all the economics terms that people toss around? Do you really understand how a product is made, shipped to market, priced and sold?

Do you understand the impact that the manufacturing process has on our economy? Do you understand all the factors that you must consider when you produce anything, even a simple potato chip?

It's a potato chip, yet you have to deal with government on a variety of levels and the decisions that government makes ranging from new regulations to passing laws that limit your supply of resources.

Can you read an income statement, cash flow statement, balance sheet? Do you know the key financial ratios? Do you know the difference between simple economics terms like elastic and inelastic? The real cost of hiring an employee? What the heck is the difference between a stock and bond? What are demand shifters? Supply shifters? How do you rally employees?

How do you deal with cancer scares, environmental regulations, slow sales; how do you introduce new products; why are entrepreneurs crucial to our economy; what is the Multiplier

Effect; is hiring more cops a good economic move? How do you really market a product to stay in business; how do you survive as a small fish in a big pond?

A lot of questions. But these can all be answered and your economics literacy greatly improved just by following a simple potato chip from the field to the production plant to the market.

And that is what this book does. The people at Golden Flake talked to us and talked to us, they opened their doors to us and shared everything they had to do to sell one potato chip.

And just by following a potato chip from the field to the shelf, this book answers the above questions and more. And each answer is designed to increase your economics literacy, to understand how the world of business really works.

Welcome to *Potato Chip Economics* where you will learn about marketing and production and economics and government regulations and cancer scares and all sorts of economics stuff no one has ever explained to you before in a way so that you can understand how the real world works.

Lesson One

The World of Chips – Buying raw materials, making chips, transporting the chips, marketing the chips…

Chapter 1

The Real World of Raw Materials or "You can't cook a thought."

Or – Why do economics professors rattle on and on about raw materials?

I saw all the people hustling early in the morning to go into the factories and the stores and the office buildings, to do their job, to get their checks. But ultimately, it's not office buildings or jobs that give us our checks. It's the soil. The soil is what gives us the real income that supports us all.
– Ed Begley, Jr.

Introduction: In every basic economics class, we have heard the mantra of raw materials. But I think few students, heck, few adults, really understand the crucial importance of raw materials.

A quick example – when you turn on a light switch, you expect that light switch to work. You give it no further thought. But someone had to dig the coal out of the ground; someone had to transport that coal across thousands of miles, just to deliver it to your local power plant, where they need the coal to make steam, to turn the turbines to produce electricity. The turbines are made out of steel, which is made out of iron ore, which is dug out of the ground. The turbines make electricity, which cruises through the copper wires in your house.

Ah yes, copper to make the wires, copper, which again is dug out of the ground. The point is simple: from the copper wires, to the wood in your house to the steel in your car, to the gas which powers your car, everything must be dug out of the earth somewhere. Lights don't just go on because you flip a switch. Every material involved in that process of bringing you light and

8

power was dug out of the ground at some point.

Let's apply that to the subject of this book. Potato chips. Again raw materials are the most elementary of any manufacturing process. Without a potato you can't make chips. Sounds simple. Dig potatoes out of the ground and make chips. No – it is way more complicated than that; just like every facet of economics, things can go wrong and you must have back-up plans, and relationships and the right potatoes and the right storage...

And a 'by-the-way moment', the Latin term for potatoes is Solanum tuberosum. And the potato and the sweet potato are not related.

Come on – it's just potatoes!

Quote: Money is the root of all evil, and yet it is such a useful root that we cannot get on without it any more than we can without potatoes.

– *Louisa May Alcott*

How hard can it be to make potato chips? Buy the potatoes, stick them in the fryer, bag them up, throw them into a box, stick them on a truck and deliver them to the store.

However, as you may suspect by now, this book is intended to teach you how to succeed in the real world of business and how to expect the unexpected and how to deal with it.

Let's look at one of the most basic raw materials that go into making a potato chip. Potatoes. How many potatoes? Golden Flake uses over 100 million pounds of potatoes a year and it takes about four pounds of potatoes to make one bag of chips. (The average American eats five pounds of potato chips a year.)

When you make any food product, it is hard to predict what your costs of raw materials will be. If you make a watch, you can pretty much predict how much it will cost you to buy each component for that watch. And those components do not vary from year to year.

But look at potato chips. They depend on potatoes (okay, I know that is obvious, but bear with me), and a whole range of things can happen to the potato supply ranging from diseases to legislation to bad luck. And that makes it hard to predict each year how much potatoes will cost you.

Oh – those variable costs!

To toss out an economics term, potatoes represent 'variable costs', costs which change from year to year, as opposed to fixed costs, which stay 'fixed' every year. A fixed cost might be the mortgage on your building, the payments you make on your fryers, or a fleet of trucks.

So your challenge becomes trying to control the costs of potatoes, because even if the costs increase, you can't increase the price on a bag of chips; you still have to sell those chips for about two bucks a bag. Of course, you could increase the price of your chips and happily go bankrupt, as your competitors did not get the memo to increase their prices.

How much can the price of potatoes change? In June 2008 they were $10.37 per 100 pounds; a year earlier they were $7.75.

That is an increase of 34%. Can you imagine making a car and the raw materials for the car increase 34%? Yet potato chip manufacturers have to deal with that 34% increase without passing it onto the consumer. Can you imagine if the price of chips went up 34% in a year?

You would have a tough decision to make. Should I put a gallon of gas in my car or buy a bag of chips.

What is going on here? Where are my cheap potatoes?

But why does the price of raw materials, potatoes, fluctuate so much?

A number of factors affect the price of potatoes and many factors are out of the chip maker's control. This means, and this could be the key lesson for any businessperson, that you must adjust, adjust and adjust again. Or as that great American philosopher, Dolly Parton, once said, "We cannot direct the wind, but we can adjust our sails."

Anyway, while we take for granted that we will always have potato chips, let's look at the many factors that snack food companies fight against every day, just to get the potatoes to make the chips.

One key reason for a 34% price increase in potatoes was that flooding destroyed a number of acres of new crop potatoes, up to 50 to 70% in Missouri and other areas.

Hmm – it can't be good when the materials you need to make your product are wiped out by flooding and you still must get chips to the shelf to keep your employees employed and your customers happy.

Remember, there isn't any revenue if you don't sell any chips.

But hey, despite the occasional flood, what else could happen?

Well, the total US acres of potatoes planted has been reduced by 10% from 2007. Why? The government has mandated that 25% of the entire corn crop must be used to make ethanol and not food.

And if you are a farmer with half a brain and the government is paying you to grow corn and not potatoes, you are going to grow corn.

Opportunity costs – a cool economics term

Quote: Four things come not back – the spoken word, the sped arrow, the past life, and the neglected opportunity.
– *Arabian Proverb*

Let me sneak in another economics term here – Opportunity Costs. Everything has an opportunity cost. If you watch TV for an hour, you have lost the opportunity to read a book, eat dinner, and play catch with your son.

If you grow corn on your 100 acres of land, you have lost your opportunity to grow potatoes on that same land.

We obviously choose what is more desirable by the choices we make.

You think the opportunity to watch TV for an hour is more profitable than reading a book. You may argue that you don't think that way at all, but you had the opportunity to read a book or watch TV. Your choice, your action to watch TV tells me what you think is more profitable.

All resources are scarce and if you grow corn on your land instead of potatoes, you have chosen the 'opportunity' that offers the best profit. Unfortunately – and this could lead into a long, long discussion of free markets, but – your decision to grow corn was not influenced by what the consumer needs; it was decided by a government program to offer you more money for growing corn. Which kind destroys the basic law of supply and demand.

Which, believe it or not, leads us back to potatoes.

What could happen?

Quote: The only good luck many great men ever had was being born with the ability and determination to overcome bad luck.

– *Channing Pollock*

So to recap, what can happen to the potatoes you need for your chips?

Hmm, so far the demand for corn has increased, limiting the land available to grow potatoes and there was that flooding which wiped out 70% of the Missouri potato crop.

What else can happen? Well, farmers want to make a profit. What could they be thinking?

And in recent years, the cost of producing potatoes has increased. Think of all the costs associated with growing potatoes, which include higher land, fuel, equipment, fertilizer and storage costs. And the higher cost of everything translates into the higher cost of potatoes, which affects that bag of chips on the shelf.

Think about that. Who thinks about the cost of fertilizer?

Heck, I don't wake up at three in the morning worrying about fertilizer, and I hope you don't either. But every time you eat a bag of chips and every time that bag of chips increases in price, you are paying for the increasing costs of fertilizer.

So if you run a potato chip company, fertilizer must factor into your business thinking. I could say that is no B.S., but that would be a bad pun.

Tariffs and chips — what's the connection?

Quote: Tariffs that save jobs in the steel industry mean higher steel prices, which in turn mean fewer sales of American steel products around the world and losses of far more jobs than are saved.

— *Thomas Sowell*

Recently Hostess, the maker of Twinkies and other gourmet foods, went out of business. Was it due to bad management? Actually it was due to tariffs. A news item stated:

Economists say high sugar prices tied to US trade tariffs were a big reason Hostess was struggling, but a Mexican company could be a lifeline for Twinkies because it would be able to take advantage of access to lower-priced sugar in Mexico.

Tariffs can also raise the price of potatoes.

American potato farmers sell a lot of potatoes to Mexico. And Mexico and other foreign markets get angry at us. I know, hard to believe that some country might get angry at us, but let's say Mexico does. And they stick a tariff on American-grown potatoes. It has happened and can happen again.

So if you are in Mexico buying potatoes, what are you going to buy? The cheaper Mexican grown potatoes or the ones with the extra tariff tax on them. Of course, you are going to buy the cheaper potatoes.

No big deal, but a Mexican tariff on potatoes can cost American farmers $80 million a year. And if they aren't making that $80 million in Mexico, they will raise prices to Americans. And that can hurt, especially if you buy millions of pounds a potatoes a year; for instance if you own a potato chip factory, like Golden Flake.

You can thank Congress

Quote: Nothing is better than the unintended humor of reality.
– *Steve Allen*

Another quick detour, as we return to a favorite theme of this book. How one action leads to another action and affects you as a businessperson.

Mexico did impose a tariff on potatoes and it was not the snack company's fault or the poor guy growing potatoes.

The tariff was imposed, costing potato farmers over $80 million a year, and forcing Golden Flake to face rising potato costs because of some obscure act of Congress.

A news story on what happened might read like this:

Fruits and vegetables – including potatoes – are the most common items on the list of 90 products hit with tariffs as of today, as Mexico retaliated against a US decision to block Mexican trucks from traveling north of a commercial zone along the border.

Potato growers alone could lose an annual market of $80 million.

Mexico acted after Congress inserted in a budget bill a provision to halt funding for a program that let a limited number of Mexican trucks deliver goods throughout the US.

Growing houses, not potatoes

Quote: A lot of people stop short. They don't actually die but they say, "Right I'm old, and I'm going to retire," and then they dwindle into nothing. They go off to Florida and become jolly boring.

– *Mary Wesley*

Okay, so now we have tariffs, congressional actions, floods, the costs of growing potatoes, better money growing corn, less land to grow potatoes all affecting you, as you sit in your office at Golden Flake, trying to keep the costs of potatoes down, so you can keep selling chips at a two bucks a bag.

Can it get more complicated? Of course it can. That is the challenge of doing business in the real world. Just when you ask, "What could happen?" it happens.

Potato chip makers follow the potato chip market from south to north, which makes sense when you think about it. They aren't growing any potatoes in North Dakota in the winter, but they are growing potatoes in Florida.

So you buy your first crop of potatoes in Florida. But Florida is one of the fastest growing states, and will grow even faster when 75 million baby boomers all cross the Florida border at once. Okay that might be a small exaggeration, but think about this.

To accommodate the growing Florida population, you need more houses, and you need land to build houses on. And the last time we checked, no one is making any more land. There is a limited supply of land (notice how cleverly we snuck in the basic rule of supply and demand). So where do you get the land to build houses on?

Potato farms.

And if you are a potato farmer and someone offers you a

million bucks or more for your land and you no longer have to grow potatoes all day, what would you do?

In short, the housing boom in Florida has impacted potato growers and Florida has lost a lot of potato farms.

For every action, another set of reactions. Will this ever end?

Quote: Business, more than any other occupation, is a continual dealing with the future; it is continual calculation, an instinctive exercise in foresight.

– *Henry R. Luce*

Okay, I know I am repeating myself here, but the beauty of business is that there are so many layers to it and one reaction causes another reaction.

Consider this.

Your neighbor sells his farm and a developer comes in and builds houses. (Notice the concept of opportunity costs here. It is a better opportunity to use the land to grow houses and not potatoes.)

But once your neighbor sells his land, you as a farmer have a whole new set of issues to deal with.

For some reason the new residents want clean water to drink – heck it is not your fault they are so picky – but you must deal with drainage issues and tougher water regulations. Plus chemical applications and spray drifts have to be carefully monitored. Come on, who wants their sweet child playing in the front yard, while toxic chemicals drift through the air, caused by the spraying of potato fields?

Also highway rights have to be worked out, so farmers can move their machinery to other fields on roads that carry more non-farm traffic. In other words, if mom and dad are commuting to the city every day, from their nice new home in the suburbs, the last thing they want is to be stuck behind some yahoo, driving his tractor to the potato fields.

Wait, even more terrible things can happen to potatoes, plus a real short history lesson

Let's think even more about potato farmers and how what happens to them affects Golden Flake and affects what you pay for that bag of chips. Look at Florida for example.

Florida can get freezing temperatures in late February or early March, which can wipe out the potato crop. How about throwing in some heavy rain, which can knock down hilled rows, which can cause root damage and sunburn.

Let's return to basics for a moment here. This book shows that business can be a challenging endeavor and you can't take anything for granted. Most textbooks say 'raw materials' and that is about all they say. But raw materials, in this instance potatoes, are never guaranteed and events can happen that can leave you scrambling to find potatoes to make chips to fill the bags that feed your customers.

But the deeper lesson here is that at times we all forget that our society depends on two acres of top soil to grow everything we eat and to grow cotton for everything we wear.

And even the smartest businessperson is at the mercy of the elements. You can crunch numbers all you want but a flood, tornado, hurricane, drought can wipe out the best-laid plans.

We often forget the potato famine that devastated Ireland. In two years Ireland lost two million people.

A quick history lesson

Quote: True the greater part of the Irish people was close to starvation. The numbers of weakened people dying from disease were rising. So few potatoes had been planted that, even if they escaped blight, they would not be enough to feed the poor folk who relied upon them. More and more of those small tenants and cottagers, besides, were being forced off the land and into a condition of helpless destitution. Ireland, that is to say, was a country utterly prostrated.

– *Edward Rutherfurd*

The Irish Potato Famine began in 1845 as leaves on potato plants suddenly turned black and curled, then rotted. An airborne fungus (phytophthora infestans), originally transported in the holds of ships traveling from North America to England, was the culprit.

Winds from southern England carried the fungus to the countryside around Dublin. Fungal spores settled healthy potato plants, multiplied and were carried by cool breezes to surrounding plants. A single infected potato plant could infect thousands more in just a few days.

And the Irish starved. Before the famine, Irish families ate an average of ten pounds of potatoes a day. But the bright side, if there was one, is that the Irish gave us a great nickname for potatoes. The term 'spud' comes from the Irish name for a type of spade used for digging potatoes.

So what's with all this history?

Okay – nice history lesson, but what does it have to do with potatoes today? Well diseases that attack potatoes have not disappeared, and our food supply is never as safe as we like to pretend it is.

Here are just some of the diseases that can ruin a potato farmer's day. Or year. Or decade.

Alfalfa mosaic virus
Andean potato mottle virus
Arracacha virus B - Oca strain
Beet curly top virus
Cucumber mosaic virus
Eggplant mottle dwarf virus

Potato aucuba mosaic virus
Potato black ringspot virus
Potato deforming mosaic virus
Potato latent virus
Potato leafroll virus
Potato mop-top virus
Potato rugose mosaic
Potato stem mottle
Potato spindle tuber
Potato yellow dwarf virus
Potato yellow mosaic virus
Potato yellow vein virus
Potato yellowing virus
Potato virus A
Potato virus M
Potato virus S
Potato virus T
Potato virus U
Potato virus V
Potato virus X
Potato virus Y
Solanum apical leaf curling virus
Sowbane mosaic virus
Tobacco mosaic virus
Tobacco necrosis virus
Tobacco rattle virus
Tobacco streak virus
Tomato black ring virus
Tomato mosaic virus
Tomato spotted wilt virus
Tomato yellow mosaic virus
Wild potato mosaic virus
Aster yellows
Witches'-broom

BLTVA
Aerial tubers
Air pollution injury
Black heart
Blackspot bruise
Elephant hide
Hollow heart
Internal brown spot = heat necrosis
Jelly end rot
Physiological leaf roll
Psyllid yellows
Shatter bruise
Skinning
Stem-end browning

Dexter in the lab!

Quote: They that die by famine, die by inches.
— *Matthew Henry*

Every year scientists are working to stop the latest potato disease. So far, they have been able to stop diseases from spreading. But while we worry about exotic events like a meteorite hitting earth, an even more realistic scenario would involve a disease that wipes out entire crops, leading to widespread deaths from famine.

Not likely?

Consider the latest threat that scientists are working on. Scientists in South Texas are fighting a disorder in potatoes that affects the production of potato chips. So far, its cause is unknown. The disorder, called zebra chip, for the dark stripes it leaves in the flesh of raw potatoes, reduces crop yields and quality. Crops have been affected in Guatemala, Mexico, Texas and as far north as Colorado. Symptoms are especially pronounced when potatoes are sliced and fried to make potato chips, causing frying plants to reject entire loads of affected potatoes. It also affects fresh market potatoes.

Okay, so what? A small potato disease. How can that make a difference? Hmm, an economic impact study showed that, left unabated, losses from zebra chip could cost 100 million dollars in lost business in Texas and almost 1,000 jobs.

1,000 Jobs???

Wait a minute – we have a disease that could cost over 100 million dollars in Texas alone and cost the state of Texas over 1,000 jobs.

This could be serious.

I coached Babe Ruth baseball, kids in high school, and in the sixth inning, when my team was winning, we had a joke. The coaches would look at each other and say, "What could happen?"

We knew that anything could happen and often did. No lead was safe – pitchers could walk the batters, ground balls could be muffed, fly balls could be dropped, the kids could throw to the wrong base – a myriad of mistakes could pile up to cost his team the game.

And as an executive, if you are truly an executive, a manager, a leader, you know that 'anything can happen' even to the potato crop that you depend on for the chips to put into the bags to sell to the customer, so you have revenue to pay your other business expenses.

We're only trying to help

Quote: Giving money and power to governments is like giving whiskey and car keys to teenage boys.
– PJ O'Rourke

Heck what else could happen to limit the supply of potatoes?

Remember we have chatted about 'do-gooders' and how they can throw wrenches into the best-laid plans.

Jefferson Country in Alabama, where Golden Flake is located, was sued and forced to build a new sewer system because environmental groups wanted to save the rivers. That is a good impulse, but the sewer project went way over budget (crooked politicians, now in jail, took bribes – see even crooked politicians can affect your cost of doing business) and sewer rates were raised 300% driving Golden Flake's water bill through the ceiling. It can take 160 gallons of water to produce one bag of chips. Plus Golden Flake was going through 300,000 gallons of water a day. In 1998, the plant was paying $800 to $1,000 per month to Jefferson County in surcharges for dumping its 100,000 to 350,000 gallons of wastewater into the county's municipal sewer system. By 2008 that figure had escalated to $100,000 per month in surcharges for the same daily discharged wastewater flow rate, with county projections that the rate would most likely raise to $250,000 per month within the next five years. (Ah yes, stay tuned, more about this later.)

The Snail Darter

Quote: The regulators assume the public are innocents in need of protection.

– *Anon*

The point is – and again we are returning to a main point of this book – a businessperson must able to think on several layers at once, be able to anticipate and plan for levels of complexity that are found in every business, and this goes far beyond numbers and charts and graphs and financial plans.

The classic example of 'the-best-laid-plans' being undermined by do-gooders involves the case for the snail darter.

In August of 1973, a biologist discovered a small fish species, the snail darter, in the Little Tennessee River. So what harm could one small fish do? It turns out – a lot of harm.

At that time there was a major construction project; there was a dam being built which hired hundreds of workers. The Tellico Dam would create a reservoir. But the problem was, the reservoir would change the flow of the river and alter the snail darter's habitat.

Again, so what?

Well, the snail darter was on the endangered species list and the biologist and other environmental groups claimed the Tellico Reservoir would kill all the snail darters off. So, opponents of the dam invoked the Endangered Species Act to stop construction of the multimillion dollar dam (did I mentioned the dam hired lots and lots of people and no one was on the snail darter's payroll).

The Supreme Court eventually ruled in favor of the snail darter, halting construction on the Tellico Dam. And, of course, everyone filed appeals and the dam was eventually completed, after a long delay and years of layoffs for the workers.

Another detour – watch out for those weasel phrases!

Quote: How often misused words generate misleading thoughts.
– *Herbert Spencer*

The point is that the snail darter story also shows how science, politics and business are entwined. And to become a businessperson you must be competent in all three arenas.

But we digress – what do the snail darter and 'do-gooders' have to do with Golden Flake. And the supply of potatoes?

The European Union wants to ban 50 chemicals used on crops because of their potential hazard to human health. Notice the key word here "potential" – one man's potential is another man's 'you got to be kidding'.

Critics say pesticides contain ingredients, which have, in high doses, been linked to cancer and other conditions. Again, note the magic phrase "in high doses". This is a phrase that many do-gooders use, without defining what a "high dose" is. This is important because to be successful in business you have to carefully study how your opposition frames an argument and you have to be aware of 'vague' phrases that they use.

Also note that while saying, "pesticides contain certain ingredients", no one has clearly defined the ingredients.

These phrases are 'weasel phrases' and really say nothing. What is 'a high dosage'? Drinking a quart of pesticides a day?

No one knows, as your opponents never clearly define the term, but they know that if you throw the word cancer into a sentence, people will focus on the word cancer and ignore the weasel phrase 'high dosage' that precedes it.

Heck, a high dosage of anything will kill you. A 'high dosage' of water is called drowning.

Quickly back to weasel phrases, which like the phrase 'high dosage' are vague, but powerful enough to stir up public sentiment against your product or service.

Another commonly used 'weasel phrase' is "a growing body of evidence shows that…" Really, a "growing body of evidence"? To paraphrase that old Wendy catch-phrase – "show me the beef" – please don't say a "growing body of evidence", just 'show me the data'.

Of course, if you have no data, it is much easier to say, "A growing body of evidence", "Clearly…", "There is evidence that" or "Studies show…"

Note that in these vague phrases, no one is showing you the data.

Back to the main event

Quote: Government in the US today is a senior partner in every business in the country.
– *Norman Cousins*

Back to the main event of this chapter, the value of raw materials, which in Golden Flake's case are potatoes. What else can limit the supply of potatoes?

Think government regulations. Playing upon unnecessary fears and playing to a population, who has little scientific literacy, the government can pass regulations which can cause potatoes to be in limited supply.

For instance, as mentioned, the EU is trying to ban certain pesticides "which in high dosages might possibly..." Now banning these pesticides sounds good in theory, but can cause a drastic drop in the supply of potatoes.

Pests already, despite the use of pesticides, destroy 20–40% of all the food cultivated in Europe every year. European farmers predict that if you ban certain pesticides you could lose 60% of the potato crop.

All because of a cancer scare with no evidence to back it up.

Oh Yes – A Small Storage Challenge

Quote: Simple solutions seldom are. It takes a very unusual mind to undertake analysis of the obvious.

– Alfred North Whitehead

So far, we have discussed only a few of the things which can happen to potatoes and why, even in our advanced economy, we can't take any raw material, even a potato, for granted.

Now if Farmer Brown grows a thousand acres of potatoes, that really does not help Golden Flake unless Farmer Brown grows what is known as a chipping potato.

Golden Flake wants potatoes with low sugar content. Golden Flake needs potato chips that are well, golden. Hence the name. And no one will buy burned potato chips. When you fry a potato slice, the sugars in the potato are what make the chip turn brown. Too much sugar and you are looking at chips that are burned.

Golden Flake can't have that, so they buy special chipping

potatoes which have less than 3% sugar in them. The low sugar content means that that the potatoes won't burn when being fried and it also means they won't rot in storage. Too much sugar causes potatoes to rot quickly.

Which, of course, leads us to one more thing that can destroy potatoes before Golden Flake can even buy them. Potatoes have to be stored before the farmer takes them to Golden Flake and Golden Flake has to store them before they cook the potatoes.

Come on, how complicated can it be to store potatoes. Actually, storing potatoes is a relativity new science.

In the 1930s, potatoes were stored in underground root cellars that were highly susceptible to condensation that damaged the crop. Farmers knew that this problem could be resolved by ventilation, but – whoops – ventilation caused the potatoes to shrink. It actually took significant state and federal research to design above-ground storage warehouses that actually protected potatoes in storage.

Well, as you have realized by now, nothing in business is easy, even storing potatoes for Golden Flake chips.

You just can't throw the potatoes in a storage shed, like the one you have behind your house. They would mold and rot and do all kinds of nasty things, making it impossible to make chips out of them.

The potatoes are stored in specially designed warehouses where the temperature, relative humidity, oxygen and carbon dioxide are monitored and controlled to specific conditions, depending on the chipping variety, to maximize the storage life span of the potatoes. In short, the potatoes are not unlike fine art, which is protected in art museums by precise climate control.

As I mention, unlike the shed out back, potato storage areas use the latest technologies to minimize sugar content. Remember, too much sugar and the potato rots.

The farmers and then Golden Flake must store the spuds in a warehouse which has a temperature ranging from 48–52°F

(8.9–11.1°C) and is controlled to permit approximately 18 to 21 cubic feet per minute (cam) of air per ton of potatoes. The relative humidity is maintained at 90 to 95% to reduce shrinkage, pressure bruising, and loss of tuber texture.

Wow, are you impressed? All of that just to store potatoes.

The point is, if the potato crop survives the growing season and is not destroyed by natural disasters, then the potatoes must survive storage and transportation in specially refrigerated trucks and then storage again.

Finally!

Freezes, floods, tariffs, increased cost of fertilizers, housing developments, more corn, fewer potatoes, banning pesticides, heck what else could happen to your cost of raw materials? After all they are just potatoes and it can't be that tough to buy them at a decent level so you can still sell your potato chips for two bucks a bag.

The Real World of Golden Flake: The executives share their knowledge
Tracking raw materials

Everything is connected.

We can tell you the weather forecast in Brazil which is important because of commodities.

South American commodity prices have an influence on North American commodity prices. Argentina had an excellent soybean and corn bean crop down there this year and the federal government down there decided they were going to go ahead and tax soybean and corn farmers. They were going to tax the farmers more if they were going to export the crops, because the government wanted to keep the prices low at home.

So the farmers said, "Fine we will just keep everything on the farm," and they wouldn't sell any corn or soybeans.

Finally the government relented, but for a period of six to eight weeks, while the farmers withheld corn and soybeans, it really put pressure on the North American commodity market and the prices went up.

We know pork bellies, corn, wheat, potatoes, all of the world markets; commodity markets are no longer just domestic. The last 25 years it is much more global. We know when China buys. If they buy a lot of corn, the corn prices jump.

We have to have corn, so we have to take a more conservative approach to that. We try to have contracts with certain farmers that are not affected by global markets.

– *David Jones*

Acts of God or Hedging your bets

Our most volatile commodity is potatoes because there are no old potatoes.

There are certain times of years what is being grown in South Florida is it. And you don't want flood, freeze, hurricanes. If a crop in South Florida gets wiped out – what do you do?

And we did have a bad spring in Missouri with the flooding and an early frost; first time in a long time, there was a period of two weeks, where there were no potatoes.

There is an act of God clause in that these farmers do not have to supply potatoes. If they can't produce potatoes, where are they going to find them to supply us?

But that is why we are a snack food company and not a potato chip company. We have decreased our dependence on potato chips, even though they are still 45 to 50% of the business. In those time periods where you have few potatoes, you push the other items heavier and choose select sizes and flavors of potato chips and put them out there.

You make do for a while because you just can't just ignore your customers. You can't say, "Oh I am sorry, for the next

three weeks we not going to have this at all." But it does become difficult, but that is part of what we do.
– *Mark McCutcheon*

One potato, two potato, three potato, four...

Everybody else's business always looks easy. I say, "You have to do it."

Then it is not as easy as you think it is.

People say, "Potato chips. My goodness. You don't hardly put anything in the bag and charge me so much for it."

What they don't see is that 80% of the potato went up the stack in the form of steam. About 25% of the weight in the bag came from the potato. A potato is 75% water.

We have to take potatoes grown by different farmers in different states and different soils and different climate conditions, different moistures, and take these numerous different characteristics and make a potato chip so that the consumer does not know where it came from.

You have to do it winter, spring, summer, fall, all the time. You expect the same outstanding white, no brown, tasty, crispy wonderful product. And that is the goal of Golden Flake: take potatoes from Florida or North Dakota or Canada or wherever, and make the same potato chip when the potatoes are not exactly the same.

You have to have faith in God tremendously when you are a farmer or in the snack food business where you are using all agricultural products. You cannot control the climate and obviously we are affected by it. Some years, the weather is terrific and the crops are terrific. Some years the crops get damaged in one area and it gets carried over to all the rest of the areas.

For example, a bad Florida crop in the springtime typically puts pressure on the source of the potatoes we use and that pressure continues, even if there are good crops along the way, 'cause you have gotten behind.

And varieties. You have to keep breeding varieties. The government has a hand in this, through the USDA; you have to keep researching breeding varieties that will grow in different soils and are free of defects and bugs and wilts and all the things that cause potato crops to fail. And you have to keep finding varieties that will produce a yield that a farmer can make a living out of.

Another thing that people in our industry have to worry about, where is the potato grown? With fuel, energy costs so high these days, it costs a tremendous amount to move raw potatoes from the field to where they are processed.

If you could grow them next door all year, it would be wonderful, but you can't. Actually Golden Flake buys potatoes all the way from Florida to Canada. We used to buy some Arizona potatoes, but it's a long way from Arizona. The freight just got to be atrocious.

And you want the right potatoes. You want a round white potato with shallow eyes so you can have a good smooth potato to peel, but you have to have potatoes with a low sugar content, because sugars cook brown. That's why people think you burn the chips, but they had hot sugar in them and no they are not burned, the sugar just cooks brown – so a high concentration of sugar in the potato causes you to have brown chips. So to eliminate the sugar, you want starchy potatoes which cook white.

When we buy potatoes we work through a broker, an agent – call them what you want to – they work on our behalf, they aren't just going out, working on their own, buying from the farmer and selling to us. We are very involved with the farmers, we know the farmers. I have met farmers all throughout the states. I used to buy potatoes; that was one of my first jobs at Golden Flake.

– *Wayne Pate*

Buying potatoes

We deal with Jack Rubin and Son. Jack is dead, son is in his 80s, they have been handling our potato needs for many, many years. I suspect 50, 60 years. They contract on our behalf with growers. We have a say in who they contract with.

We know the growers and we just don't depend on the Rubins. We go visit the growers, they know who we are. They know what we expect them to ship to us and they know when we say that their potato doesn't meet quality specs, they know we are not trying to mess them up. We give them straight answers.

We contract directly with growers for specific varieties. We specify that we want so many hundred weights of a specific variety which we know the farmer will grow for us.

A grower knows how much it costs him to produce potatoes. He expects to make a certain yield on his acres and he has to base his contract terms on that.

And we know what we can sell a bag of chips for, so we can agree with the grower on a set contract price.

We stay away from the commodity market because in the commodity market prices go up and down, prices can change daily.

We can't play that game. We can't change price very often on potato chips. It is difficult because you have your pre-printed bags and all of that. With the printed price on the bag, we have to stabilize prices.

So we have to deal with growers directly and they know they can sell what they produce to Golden Flake at a fair price.

– *Wayne Pate*

How relationships pay off

There have been years where there have been shortages of potatoes, and that is why we know the farmers. We build a good relationship with our growers. Golden Flake has always tried to be a great company to work for, to deal with from a customer or a supplier perspective.

We are nice to all of them and dependable. We do what we say. You work on that relationship with growers, so they know we are not trying to cheat them. They know that we will work with them to use their potatoes.

So because of that good relationship, some years when the crops have been very short, and dishonest growers would be tempted to go out and harvest their crops and sell at a much higher price than the contract, our growers don't.

The relationship is critical; of course they know that we will be there good years, bad years. So we have been able, by and large, for our growers to dig for us, honor our contracts and supply whatever potatoes they have.

We always have an Act of God clause in those contacts. In other words, through an Act of God, weather and the crop not being produced in the amount expected, he is not obliged to sell us what he could not produce.

Because of these relationships, there are very few times that we have been out of potatoes. There have been a few times when we have stopped production or cut back on certain items for a short period of time because you can't make a potato chip out of a thought.

Sometimes we have gone as far as Canada to buy potatoes, but we don't normally contract in those areas; but we have had to when the potato supplies in our regular areas have been short. I have walked around potato farms in New Brunswick.

Basically our potato supplies come from Tampa Bay, Florida. The main Florida potato growing area is around Hastings by the Saint John River; we used to use about 20 million pounds of Florida potatoes. We started in late March or April or May, then we moved up to Alabama.

We use very few Alabama potatoes now. They have problems in the soil, and diseases and that type of thing, so we started buying Missouri and North Carolina potatoes, so typically we buy in June and July – Missouri and North Carolina potatoes.

Then we move up to Wisconsin and Minnesota and North Dakota and Michigan. And we buy some from Indiana.

Typically we will go as far north as above Grand Forks, North Dakota. Probably fifty, sixty miles north of Grand Forks in the Red River Valley of North Dakota.

– *Wayne Pate*

The power of diversification

We decided years ago, when I went to work for the company in 1968, the majority of the products sold were chips and we decided that we had to be more diversified.

We had to get into more items and one of the first things I did at Golden Flake was to get the pork skin business under federal inspection and get us into the corn chip and the tortilla chip business and make cheese curls.

I helped develop all the products and the idea was to diversify so we were a broad range snack food company and not just a potato chip company. Because of the weather and other conditions affecting potatoes, it can be shaky at times to be just a potato chip company. Corn can be stored. You can use last year's crop of corn to make this year's corn and tortillas chips.

– *Wayne Pate*

The importance of storage

Plus potatoes have a very short life and you have a limited time you can store them – and I designed and built the potato chip storage facility at Golden Flake, but the potato is a living, breathing organism. It has to have oxygen; if you put it in the light, it will turn green; if you don't spray sprout inhibitor on it and if you put it in the dark it will sprout.

The chemistry of a potato changes if you change the temperature more than three degrees. It will convert starches to sugars; if you get it too cold, it starts to convert. And you don't want that.

Potatoes are like people. If you live in Rochester, New York, you put on a lot of clothing because it gets cold and you need protection. If you go to Florida, light clothing – you don't need that much clothing. Potatoes are that smart. Potatoes grown in Florida develop thin skins; potatoes grown up North develop thick skins. Cold climates develop a thick, heavy skin.

Florida potatoes, typically, cannot be stored very long because they have thin skin and no protection, whereas Northern potatoes, if you cut them, they heal themselves, they can be preserved over long period of time.

So Northern potatoes can be stored as much as six months. Florida potatoes probably not more than a week or two. I tell you that potatoes are smart. God made them that way; they are living breathing organisms, so you have to have the right temperature, the right amount of air, the right amount of moisture. Because a potato is mostly water, if you don't keep it in a high humidity environment, the potatoes will shrivel up. You can't peel a shriveled potato very well.

We used to store 20 million pounds of potatoes at Golden Flake at the Alabama plant. I think we can store 8 to 9 million pounds at the Florida plant. Somewhere around those numbers. They keep changing and alternating the storage sometimes, they find another need for it. So it might be 18 million pounds.

– *Wayne Pate*

Storage again: You got to know what you are doing
In the fall there is a certain period of time where no potatoes

are being harvested anywhere.

Man!

Starting in October, starting when you get frost, freezing up North, frost up North changes everything, so the growers are trying to get the potatoes out of the ground and into their warehouses.

Potatoes from the Northern warehouses are shipped to our warehouses in September and October. But once a freeze comes in October all potato growing stops.

When the potatoes arrive from the farm, what we want to do is put them into a dormant state. Put them to sleep. Think about a person. When you are asleep, you do not consume much energy. When you are sleeping that is when your requirement for energy is at its very lowest. So you don't lose any weight when you are sleeping.

Potatoes are the same way. We want to put potatoes to sleep so it will not change anything. And then we want to wake it up. We do that with temperature. We have learned, we have varieties now that we can store at lower temperatures. Obviously if you can store at lower temperatures without changing the chemistry, keeping that starch from converting into sugar, you can keep the potato firmer and longer.

We used to have to store at 60 degrees. Then we got down to 55 degrees. Then we have a variety now that we can store at 50 degrees.

But we are still playing a balancing game which is crucial to protect our raw material – the potato. The temperature, the air movement, the humidity... all that has to be controlled very carefully. This is all done with computers which send warning signals to our potato manager. At his house he knows if the warehouse messes up because if a chiller or heater or anything messes up, he knows it. In the middle of the night or on the weekends.

You've got a big investment in your potatoes in your warehouse. Not only is it a big investment, but that is your source of what you are going to produce.

– *Wayne Pate*

Chapter 2

Understand the complexity of production: Why you need to know science

Our food processing, packaging, and distribution industries have made huge strides toward minimizing food losses, and today virtually 100% of the food produced at the farm now finds its way to consumers' tables. This is very different than much of the rest of the world, where as much as 50% or more of the food produced at the farm never gets to the people because it is lost to insects, microorganisms, humidity, or other factors.

– John Floros

Introduction: An ongoing theme of this book is that, by the time, you finish reading this book, you know, on a bone deep level, that even a bag of chips represents years of scientific progress and, to make that bag of chips affordable, an amazing number of factors must all be aligned. So again, this chapter is more than just the 'production of chips'; it is designed to deepen your understanding of how successful business people must keep learning and then learn some more.

A short overview: How they make chips

The potato goes through many steps before it becomes a potato chip. First the potatoes are dumped into a bath and washed. Then they are lifted to the peeler.

And we are talking one huge PEELER! It's not the little metal peeler you use in your kitchen. The peeler is a long cylinder with rollers that revolve around and around stripping the potato of its skin. The peeled potatoes then empty onto an inspection table where inspectors look for defects in the potatoes to remove.

Then the potatoes go through a slicer that features many

sharp blades held upright in a ring. In the center of this ring is a revolving plate. One by one the potatoes drop upon this revolving plate, which throws the potatoes against the revolving blades to slice the potatoes. Generally these slices are 1/20 of an inch. After being fried, and then after having salt and other seasonings added, the average potato chip is about .04 to .08 of an inch thick.

How effective are these slicers? One slicer can do 8,000 to 10,000 pounds of potatoes daily or more than two million pounds annually. How fast is that? Well, the world record for the greatest amount of potatoes peeled by five people, all slicing furiously away with standard kitchen knives for 45 minutes, is 587 pounds.

Before the slices are carried to the fryer, they are washed and dried. Hot oil and slices are then put in the fryer together. While cooking the chips, the hot oil pushes them from the back of the trough to the front where they are carried off by conveyor belt.

A conveyor lifts the chip out of the oil and they are salted, seasoned and inspected. They are packaged. And another fact you cannot live without. One packing machine packs 18,000 50g bags a day and between 5,000 to 6,000 150g bags a day. A 50g bag contains about 60 chips.

And in our quest to show that business is all about details and how details can make the difference, Golden Flake and every other chip maker worries about breakage. No one wants a bag containing not potato chips, but potato crumbs.

In short for Golden Flake and other chip producers, preventing breakage is a primary goal. That is why they have installed safeguards at various points in the manufacturing process to decrease the chances for breakage. The heights that chips fall from conveyer belts to fryers have been decreased. Plastic conveyer belts have been replaced with wide mesh stainless steel belts. These allow only the larger chips to travel to the fryers and the smaller potato slivers to fall through the mesh.

Maillard Reaction: Hey – Chemistry Class is Important

Quote: The most exciting phrase to hear in science, the one that heralds new discoveries, is not "Eureka!" but "That's funny..."

– *Isaac Asimov*

To be a success in business, every student must take a chemistry class. Because when you are dealing with production processes, you have to know your chemistry. Or at least have a good sense of what is happening.

For instance, Golden Flake chips are golden because of the Maillard Reaction. Not a fancy name, but it was named after Louis-Camille Maillard, a French chemist, who studied why things turn brown when you cook them.

Which sounds obvious, but actually there are a lot of chemical reactions when something is cooked and Golden Flake's entire chip empire depends on GOLDEN chips, not burned ones. So the Maillard reaction is crucial to their success.

A quick overview of the Maillard reaction is that certain foods, think potatoes here, contain carbohydrates in the form of sugars while others contain amino acids in the form of proteins. These sugars and proteins exist side-by-side in potatoes.

The Maillard reaction occurs when you cook something. The carbon molecules contained in the sugars or carbohydrates combine with the amino acids of the proteins. The result of this chemical reaction is the Maillard reaction. Things turn brown. Like chips turn brown when they are cooked in oil.

Okay – that sounds obvious that things turn brown when you cook them, but when you are striving for the same color of brown EVERY time, things get complicated. You cannot have a bag of half-brown chips, brown chips and burned chips.

Actually, and again this is very scientific, a good way to remember the Maillard reaction is to remember this saying: "The sugar and protein all react until brown."

Yes, despite our best efforts, science does march forward.

Sugar, sugar, honey, honey

Actually honey has nothing to do with it, but sugar has every-thing to do with the proper color of a Golden Flake chip. The lower the sugar, the browner the chip. The higher the sugar content, the Maillard Reaction kicks in, the sugar combines with the proteins and you get a burned chip.

Golden Flake wants a chip with no more than 10% sugar.

But other factors can determine if a chipping potato has too much sugar. When the farmer pulls the potato from the ground, it might have the right percent of sugar. But improper storage or too long in storage gives the potato a chance to make more sugar. And that ain't good, which is why storage is so important and Golden Flake spent millions to ensure it had the proper storage facilities.

Gravity matters

Let's talk about gravity. No – not the kind that keeps you glued to the earth. The specific gravity of a potato.

When you choose a chipping potato, you want one with as much solid matter as possible, and with as little water as possible,

And even the best potatoes, especially designed to produce potato chips, are 75% water.

And when you drive by the Golden Flake factory, you almost always see steam coming out of a stack. As the Golden Flake executives say, "That's our profits going up in steam."

In fact, that is why many snack companies like corn chips. They can use 100% of the corn they buy to make chips. They can only use 25% of the potatoes they buy to make chips.

But you still try to get the most out of your raw material. Especially when paying to have potatoes shipped clear across the country. You want to at least use 25% of the potato to make chips.

And that is where the term specific gravity comes into play.

Specific gravity means the amount of solid matter, dry matter in a potato that you can actually cook and turn into a chip. The higher the specific gravity, the better the potato is to cook. The lower the specific gravity – not so good. You increase your production costs by having to drive the water out of the potato and by having less potato to cook.

High specific gravity potatoes also absorb less oil when cooking. That is good as that means a crispy and not a soggy chip.

If the potato has too much water, a low specific gravity, the water is replaced by the oil during cooking. Thus you get a chip with too much grease.

Determining specific gravity

Hey, sooner or later we had to throw in a formula. Business people love formulas and who are we to disappoint the business majors reading this book.

The point is that everything in business must have a process. There must be a way to measure; what you can't measure, you can't manage.

And raw material is no different. Golden Flake spends millions a year on potatoes, growing potatoes, digging potatoes, shipping potatoes, storing potatoes.

So you must have a measurement to ensure that the potatoes you receive have a high specific gravity and that they contain enough dry matter to make it worthwhile to ship clear across the country.

In short, potatoes with high specific gravity, and thus higher solids, make better chipping potatoes than those with high water content. Total solids should be in the range of 20% to 23%, which equates to specific gravities of 1.080 to 1.095, respectively. The highest-quality potatoes typically have more than 25% total solids, which equates to a specific gravity of 1.105 or higher. If this paragraph didn't put you to sleep, nothing will and you are to be admired for your perseverance.

One more fact. Many chip makers will not accept potatoes if the specific gravity is below 1.080. This is a fact you can toss out at parties to amuse your friends and amaze your relatives. Of course, odds are you won't be invited back to any other parties.

Yet, the burning question remains and I know you will have many sleepless nights unless it is answered. How do you determine specific gravity? Oh boy, a formula and a chart are just ahead.

Formula and charts, Oh my!

Actually it is not complicated to determine specific gravity. The most common method is *the weight in air/ weight in water method*. Selected sample units are first weighed in air and then the same unit is re-weighed suspended in water. Specific gravity can then be calculated using the following formula:

Specific gravity = Weight in air / (Weight in air − Weight in water)

The total solids of the potatoes can be estimated from the calculated specific gravity measurements using the following table:

Specific gravity	Percent total solids
1.072	19.0
1.074	19.4
1.076	19.8
1.078	20.3
1.080	20.7
1.082	21.1
1.084	21.6
1.086	22.0
1.088	22.4
1.090	22.8
1.092	23.2
1.094	23.7

Of course, I highly doubt you will spend your weekends determining the specific gravity of potatoes. But the point is that everything is more complicated than it seems, and specific gravity, although a dissertation on it is a good way to bore your friends, is very important to Golden Flake. How important is specific gravity to Golden Flake's profits? In general, each 0.005 increase in specific gravity increases chip yield by about 1.0% and reduces oil content by 1.7%. And when you make millions of chips a year those percentages add up.

Manufacturing chips and starch and chicken feed and...

Quote: Obviously, the highest type of efficiency is that which can utilize existing material to the best advantage.

– *Jawaharlal Nehru*

Okay, we have discussed the importance of raw materials. And basically in business you want to maximize the use of your raw material. And that is why at Golden Flake nothing is wasted. The starch driven from the potatoes during washing and cooking is separated into a vat and that starch is sold to paper companies to make paper. At the end of the cooking line, the chips that are too small fall through the conveyor and are sold as chicken feed.

Golden Flake has spent thousands getting the right potato peelers. You want to peel as little of the potato as possible. That gives you more to cook. Ideally Golden Flake wants to lose only 1% of the potato to peeling.

Then slicing is important. In fact it is critical. Every chip must be sliced the exact same thickness, so they all fry exactly the same and they all come out with the famous golden color of Golden Flake.

That leads us to frying, which is all part of the Golden Flake potato chip manufacturing line that includes a sequence of operations: cleaning, peeling and spotting, slicing, washing, frying, seasoning, and packaging.

And that brings us to frying the chips

Frying in oil is basically a dehydration process: Oil drives water out of fried food. Remember that potatoes used for chipping are ideally about 75% water (25% total solids), and need to be reduced to about 1.5% water. In general, 100 pounds of potatoes yields about 25 pounds of potato chips.

This includes the weight of the oil absorbed, which is about 35% of the finished weight of the chips. Yes, you heard that right. A potato chip is about 35% fried oil. Kind of makes you want to pick up a bag on the way to the gym. Okay – maybe not.

The exposure of a potato chip to hot oil during frying has several effects:

- Starch, the predominant food component of potato (up to 99.5% of dry weight), is gelatinized, thus rendering the potato more easily digestible.
- The water content of the slice is reduced from about 75% to about 1–2%, resulting in a desirable crisp texture and stability from microbiological spoilage.
- Cooking oil is absorbed into the chip, enhancing flavor and texture.

But remember our lessons about the value of raw materials, and how you want to get the most of your investment.

Well frying is an area where things can go wrong.

Here's why.

First, Golden Flake must control and monitor frying time and temperature to produce uniform, high-quality chips. To do that, one production line must be dedicated to potato chips.

Why?

Golden Flake manufactures a variety of snack foods, and dedicates fryer lines to one base material, i.e. one line for potato slices and the other for corn-based snacks, since oils pick up flavors from the foods they fry.

But remember our famous saying in business, "Hey what can go wrong?"

Let's look at all the variables it takes to produce perfect Golden Flake chips every time:

Moisture control – You have to make sure that your frying stops exactly when the chip has only 1–2% moisture in it. For example, a 1.4 mm thick slice at 180°C will reach this range after about 2 minutes of fry time. Why must the moisture content be so low? If moisture is above 2%, you will not have a thin, crispy chip, which is Golden Flake's trademark. Instead if the chip contains more than 3% moisture, we are talking a soggy chip. And soggy chips are worse than soggy cereal. And if you know someone who actually likes soggy cereal, I would suggest you walk away, very fast, from that person.

And, this shows how crucial it is to get the frying time down pat: if the chip contains too little moisture, below 1%, you will get a chip with excessive oiliness, dark color, and scorched flavor. In other words a greasy burned chip that tastes bad.

Oil content control – Most potato chips contain 30–40% oil. Here's an interesting fact, potato tissue only contains about 0.1% fat. So nearly all of the oil in the finished chip is due to absorption from the frying oil. But then, again, just like the moisture content, you really have to check the oil content of a chip. If the oil content rises above 40%, the chip becomes too greasy with an oil-soaked appearance.

Color control – How important is color control to Golden Flake? Look they brag about the color of their chips through the name Golden Flake. When you open a bag of Golden Flake chips, you expect to see a perfect golden chip every single time. Actually there are two components in the color of a finished chip: (a) background color, and (b) dark spots. Background color, that golden color Golden Flake lives and dies by, is due to starch caramelization and depends on how long you fry the chip, the oil temperature, and the slice thickness. Dark spots, hmm, not many people want their chips covered with dark spots, are due to the Maillard reaction of sugars with proteins that occurs during frying. As we have discussed, this is why the potatoes that Golden Flake picks are so important.

It is mainly the sugar content of the potato that determines whether dark spots will appear or not. That is why, as mentioned before, storage is so important. Sugar concentration may increase during potato storage at low temperature. Cold weather slows the breakdown of sugars to carbon dioxide and water.

Quality Control Steps

Quote: Quality is never an accident; it is always the result of high intention, sincere effort, intelligent direction and skillful execution; it represents the wise choice of many alternatives.
– *William A. Foster*

Taste samples are made from each batch throughout the production process, and the chips are checked for salt, seasoning, moisture, color, and overall flavor. Color is compared to charts that show acceptable chip colors.

Golden Flake also wants to prevent breakage. They and other companies have installed safeguards to decrease breakage. The heights that chips fall from conveyer belts to fryers have been decreased. Plastic conveyer belts have been replaced with wide mesh stainless steel belts. These allow the larger chips to travel to the fryers and the smaller potato slivers to fall through the mesh.

The Real World of Golden Flake
Manufacturing insights

Making potato chips is a messy business. The potato chips run two shifts because you have to shut the system down to filter the oil, drain the oil, wash the fryer out, and wash the starch system out.

Tortillas are somewhat easier on machinery; tortillas can

run straight around the clock because you don't have any residue coming off of those machines.

There is a whole process behind every product that we make. For instance tortilla chips which are made out of corn. When you are doing corn – the raw kernel of corn comes in, you precook it, soak it for anywhere from 10 to 12 hours, to let the moisture concentrate in it to loosen up the husks – then you mill it, sheet it, much like a cookie cutter and then fry it.
– *David Jones*

Quality control

There are two or three things that make the product turn, that make the people buy the product. First is the name and history of Golden Flake and that history stands for quality. We are very, very, very quality conscious about what we put in the bag, before it hits the street; we do checks on that, we have a whole separate QC lab that is answerable only to the president.

And the QC lab does not worry about what I tell them I want done or worry about what manufacturing goes and tells them; they worry about the quality of the product and if it does not meet standards, we do not ship it. So the consumer is reasonably assured that every bag of Golden Flake chips meets high quality standards.

I am not going to tell you that there never is a slipup. We are not going to guarantee 100% the whole time, because we can't watch every chip going in the bag; but by and large, there are very few issues that we have relative to quality, so the consumer knows from repeated purchases of the product that they can with confidence open that bag and know what is in there.

X-rays are starting to come into play – metal detectors used to be the only thing you would have and you could only look at one bag. Last week we looked at a machine that can check a whole case. The x-ray is good as it can detect any foreign matter while the metal detector could only detect metal.

Nuts, bolts and screws, and all type of things that fall apart can end up in your chips. After all, we are working with machinery. The metal detector we have been using can pick up metal, but not, for instance, rubber.

And that can be a problem. Recently one company had to recall thousands of bags of chips following the discovery of pieces of rubber in some packs produced at its manufacturing plant.

"The rubber may pose a choking hazard," the company said.

In addition to the recall, the company also had to offer refunds at the place of purchase.

The point being that any foreign substance in any bag of chips can turn into a major headache and an expensive proposition for any chip manufacturer.

– *David Jones*

Make it right

And the managers in quality control do not report to the plant manager, they report to Dave, so there is never, "Oh, that is going to hurt my numbers."

Our concept is if you would not take this home and feed it to your kids, I don't want it going out.

For instance, sometimes a tortilla can meet oil standards, the weight, the color and all of that, and still does not taste good. Something is wrong, maybe it was the humidity in the air whatever it is; let's don't put that in the sack.

We also test our competitors every week, and we chart that. We want to be the best on the market, so we look at what our competitors are doing... [he laughs] usually to make ourselves feel better.

But, every once in a while you go, "Wow, this particular plant of Frito-Lay is really stepping it up."

There was one Frito-Lay plant that always seemed to have the best potatoes, the best stuff, but for the last three years, and I don't know what their thought process is, or their management or the mindset in that plant, but the chips are terrible. The chips coming out really dropped in quality.

It really is just a scorecard that we look at from the top level on down, that we look at every week to see how we stack up against our competitors.

We even buy our product off the shelf. It's not what we do or see here at the plant, it is what the consumer sees when they open a bag of Golden Flake chips. So when QC goes out they buy our product off the shelf and at the same time they buy our competitors'. Now you are comparing apples to apples, what the consumer would see.

When we analyze a competitor's chip we look at color, defects, salt content, oil content, all those parameters that we have, including breakage, how many chips are broken in a bag?

We even get down to seeing the appearance of the bag, seals, codes...

What do you look for in breakage? There are two breakage standards, one for small bags, one for large bags and they are slightly different. The small bag breakage standard is a little more relaxed because of the way we size our potato chips down. You have a potato chip sizer which the chips go over and the little ones fall through and the big ones keep going. Then the big ones go into the big bags and the little chips go into the little bags. The little chips have a little bit more breakage because they are a little bit more fragile, so your little bag has a more relaxed standard.

In the big bag we look at breakage of less than 9%. We feel we can get out of the plant and into the marketplace if we have fewer than 9% broken chips.

And breakage might be a big chip broken in half that the consumer does not notice. We just don't want a bunch of crumbs, we do a lot of things that our loyal consumer recognizes over time; if you are a bargain hunter, you don't.

But it actually costs us. In the conveyor system there are perforated screens that take out little chips and things, and we have an optisort machine that takes out the bad and burned chips.

And the bad chips go to chicken feed, it's been fried, it has been broken, well we will not let that product go into our bags. We have been in the factories of several companies that whatever comes out of the fryer, good or bad, it's going in the bag.

The machine that takes out the bad and burned ones is just an optisort machine that says, "Okay that is not good, take it out..." Even so it still might be a good chip but appearance wise it is not, so we will kick it out.
– *Mark McCutcheon*

Scheduling Production

Unlike oil and petrochemical products, snacks can only be stored for a limited time. Plus, demand varies. We actually have just-in-time production methods. Because our production equipment is limited, we must know what snack to produce, how many, and on which production line. These are important scheduling issues.

How do we know how many chips to make?

Every route has a computer on the truck that we use to generate the tickets that we use to take the product in and check it in at the store level and then the store pays us back. Most of our accounts on the supermarket side are charge, all our 'up and down the street' businesses are cash.

In that hand-held computer, we track every item that goes

into every store every day. And our route sales team is very good at entering data into the computer accurately so that when we pull the inventory off of our trucks, we put on that ticket what goes into that store. And every afternoon, those computers call up the host computer and that host computer compiles all that data. And the next day we can look and see how much was sold on any item in any store on any route at any given time throughout that day and from that history the manufacturing division begins to build their orders so they can in turn produce enough product for the stores.

Once a week every route and our central warehouse, which houses several routes, sends in an order and that order is sent in, at least seven days in advance and is some case six days in advance, but no less than six.

And then our manufacturing section groups those orders together and from those specific orders, and along with comparing it to history, they will know how many bags of chips to make. It is a guess on manufacturing's part to make sure they have enough cooking oil in house, raw potatoes in house, salt, bags, and that is an educated guess – you have to take the history and project it to the future to make sure you have enough inventories.

They manufacture, and have ready on a certain day X, the number of cases that sales have turned in. Most of the time manufacturing is not waiting for us to turn in orders; they pretty much know because we are pretty much creatures of habit.

With the exception of promotional activity and seasonal changes – people are creatures of habit.

Our volume goes up and down a little bit and you can modify those ways, but you can't change them.

Our worse week of the year is Thanksgiving. That's because people are eating cranberry sauce, turkey, dressing, biscuits and rolls – they do not snack. Now Saturday, when all the football games come around, they are eating turkey sandwiches and potato chips.

Well, that goes into the next week and business from that point starts growing, December parties. January is still a very good month because you have all the football games and all the playoff games and Super Bowl weekend is the number one snacking occasion of the year. That is when the most snacks are consumed in a short period of time: it beats July 4th or Memorial Day weekend, it beats them all.

– Randy Bates

Cooking profits away: Potato Chip Production Basics

You get 25 pounds of potato chips from each 100 pounds of potatoes. And the reason for that, as I said, is a potato is mostly water and it goes up the stack in steam. I call it pleasant pollution. It smells wonderful and we scrubbed the oil out of it, so it is just a good puff of white steam and it smells so good, makes you want to eat a chip.

But with the potato being 75% water, you cook the water out and the water is replaced with vegetable oil. So typically a potato chip will have about 35% by weight of vegetable oil, compared to the total weight of the product.

So what is happening, you cook the water out and replace part of the water with oil, so you have potato solids, oil and light salt.

By the way, we are not a bad salt contributor. The reason people say salty snacks, all the salt is typically on the surface and you get the salt sensation immediately. So it tastes salty, but we don't have near enough salt as a lot of products – a lot of canned vegetables – because ours is all on the surface.

Most people think you can take 100 pounds of potatoes and make several truckloads of potato chips. But not so. People don't think about the steam. But we paid the same thing for the water.

– Randy Bates

Everything adds up: The importance of being efficient during production

Raw material costs an enormous amount and one thing you don't want to do is squander or waste that raw material.

You don't want to waste it when you are peeling it. Now we have peelers that do not require taking off as much as the potato as we used to have. We used to have abrasive peelers. You don't want people to have a green ring or a black ring around the chip – people look at it and say what's wrong with that – well it just might be the peel.

Most of the good things in the potato are in the outer layer around the skin. Well, obviously we can give you a more nutritious product if we don't peel all of that away.

We want to peel so we can give you a good-looking chip. People eat with their eyes. It may taste this way, but if it looks better, it tastes better. So we have had to learn to control the peeling process. And now we have peelers that reduce the loss from peeling and still produce that attractive chip that people want to buy.

Another thing, slicing is critical in the potato chip industry. You take about 20 slices per inch of potato. Our most precision piece of equipment has to be our slicers and they are very precise. So you don't create scrap and waste from slicing. And you have to get a perfect slice every time, thousands of times a day.

A 50,000 thickness chip and a 75,000 thickness chip require a different amount of time and temperature to cook. Well if you have some 75 and some 50 going through at the same time, you are going to have some undercooked and some overcooked, but neither will be correctly cooked.

– *Wayne Pate*

Chapter 3

Seasoning – and so MUCH more

The most popular potato chip flavors in the US are sour cream and onion, and barbecue. I tried to introduce broccoli and mushroom chips, but they never caught on.
– Anon

Introduction: So far, we have discussed raw materials and what can and often does go wrong. We have discussed the years of research it has taken just to find how to properly store chips. We have talked about the complications of production. As you can see, chapter upon chapter, we are building upon your business knowledge. Now we are going to talk about seasoning. You know that stuff they use on potato chips that makes them taste like salt and vinegar, or dill pickle, or barbecue... But, and I know this will come as no surprise, this simple chapter on seasoning won't be so simple after all, and will even discuss how a simple invention we take for granted, the cardboard box, revolutionized the chip business.

Down to Business: How a mistake became a $6 billion business

Bear with us. This chapter is on seasoning. And finding the right blend of flavor that will make people love your chips.

But let's take a quick tour through the developments it took to get the chip we see in the store today.

Seasoning is a part of that story.

But first, a quick trip back into potato chip history.

Most products are a work in process. There is always a newer, better product around the corner. Look at the evolution of video game, cell phones, computer and potato chips.

Potato chips reflect the history of progress and innovation that we too often take for granted in our economy.

The potato chip itself is a mistake.

In 1853, a customer at the Moon's Lake House in Saratoga Springs, New York ordered fried potatoes. He didn't like them, he thought they were too thick and sent them back to the cook.

The cook, George Crum, was pissed. And in an act of revenge, he sliced the potatoes extra thin, fried them in boiling oil until they were crispy and put some salt on them, just to teach the customer a lesson.

The act of revenge backfired. The extra thin potato slices were a big hit. They became known as Saratoga Chips and were served in restaurants in the Saratoga, New York region. Crum left the Moon Lake Inn to start his own restaurant – the Crumbs House – and put a basket of Saratoga Chips on each table. The chips soon became known up and down the East Coast of the United States.

This mistake is now a $6 billion a year business.

Progress depends on small things
Quote: Progress is impossible without change and those who cannot change their minds cannot change anything.
– *George Bernard Shaw*

Progress often depends on small things. And potato chips would have never made it big except for two more events in the 1920s.

In the 1920s, making chips was pretty low-tech. Okay, very low tech. Potatoes had to be tediously peeled and sliced by hand. But then the mechanical potato peeler was invented, paving the way for potato chips to grow from a small specialty item into a $6 billion business.

But there has to be some way of delivering the chips to the store.

And there was no way. Potato chips were stored in glass

display cases or in barrels and the chips at the bottom of the barrel were often stale and damp. In 1926, the next big step forward occurred. Laura Scudder invented the moisture-resistant potato chip bag by ironing together two pieces of wax paper. Every evening, her women employees took home sheets of wax paper and ironed them into bags.

The next day, workers would pack chips into the bags, seal the tops with warm irons and deliver them to retailers. This created a seal and kept the chips fresh until opened.

You got to love this name, her chips were called Scuds, a play on *spuds* and her surname, and they were the first to be sold in airtight sacks.

The next big thing

Now we have to go to Switzerland for the next development in this saga. A French scientist, Dr. Jacques E. Brandenberger, was sitting in a cafe when a customer spilled a glass of wine. Brandenberger had an idea – a stain-resistant tablecloth.

He started experimenting and tried to combine the flexibility of a tablecloth with the water-resistant properties of cellulose. Cellulose is the primary component in cell walls and is one of the most abundant plant fibers in nature.

No luck. The resulting fabric was too stiff to use as a tablecloth and not durable, as the plastic coating peeled off easily.

However, Brandenberger saw the coating itself was flexible, and waterproof. No luck in the tablecloth department, but he had invented a clear, flexible, plastic coating.

Cellophane – a perfect packing material for chips.

Just think that we expect potato chips to be delivered to the store every day and we can walk in and pick them up. Which leads us up to another invention. The cardboard box.

The invention of the cardboard box was another step on the path to making chips easily and cheaply available. Walk into the Golden Flake company and there are packers who do nothing but pack chips all day into cardboard boxes. As the bags of chips come off the line, they pack the chips into the boxes.

One minute they're packing small bags of chips into boxes, another minute larger bags of chips into boxes. Then barbecue chips into boxes and then sour cream and onion chips into boxes.

A quick aside. Why doesn't Golden Flake have a machine pack the chips into boxes? Because there are too many different sized bags of chips and you would have to keep adjusting the machine for each bag of chips. A human can quickly calculate which bags go into which boxes.

But back to the cardboard box. Economic progress depends on such simple ideas. The cardboard box – a simple thing, but where would we be without it? And the cardboard box is only about 100 years old. They were first used in America in 1895. Before that products were shipped in wooden crates and boxes.

Without the cardboard box, how would we ship anything? Wooden boxes would be too heavy, they would ruin the fuel economy of the trucks carrying them, and they would be awkward to load and unload.

Oh boy – more twists and turns

But how did the cardboard box become the standard for packing and shipping? Again, the story of chips is one of twists and turns. Golden Flake has the Kellogg brothers to thank for that. The advent of flaked cereals increased the use of cardboard boxes. The first to use cardboard boxes as cereal cartons were the Kellogg brothers.

And cardboard boxes are valuable. Golden Flake, forever in a battle to control costs, reuses their boxes as many as five times.

But the invention of cardboard boxes was only the first battle in getting chips to stores. We take modern packaging for granted, but actually there is a whole science behind it (see the chapter on packaging).

Finally! Seasoning!

Hey, do you think seasoned chips have been around forever? As the previous section showed, potato chips show the evolution that society and products must go through to become what we buy today.

But before we venture into the complexities of seasoning, think about this pleasant thought. When you think you are tasting flavor, you really are tasting gases.

What is flavor? Our taste buds can detect basic tastes, including salty, sweet, sour, bitter, astringent. But experts will tell you that flavor is primarily "the smell of gases being released by the chemicals you've just put in your mouth."

But back to seasoning.

It wasn't until 1920 that Frank Smith, who owned Smith's Potato Crisp Company, had the bright idea of seasoning chips by placing a twist of salt inside the bag, which the customer could apply as needed. Frank Smith originally packaged these 'seasoned' chips in greaseproof paper bags.

Hard to believe, but progress in the chip business is slow at best. Except for that twist of salt, the potato chip remained unseasoned until Joe *"Spud"* Murphy (who owned an Irish crisp company called Tayto) developed the technology to add seasoning during manufacturing in the 1950s. The potato chip was invented in 1853, so it took almost 100 years to add seasoning to chips.

Tayto was small potatoes (hey – someone had to say it) and it consisted mainly of Spud's family. Yet they produced the world's first seasoned chips – Cheese & Onion and Salt & Vinegar.

Wow – now we can season chips? This concept became a sensation and some of the biggest potato chip companies came to the Tayto company to buy the rights to use the new technology. The Tayto innovation changed the whole nature of the potato chip business.

But you can't just sprinkle seasoning on a chip and hope it

sticks.

By now you have figured out, even in the 'simple world' of potato chips, nothing is that easy.

To stay competitive, Golden Flake must consistently produce well-coated potato chip products. Well-coated means when Golden Flake puts the chips in the bag, the seasoning sticks to the chips and you don't find a bunch of naked chips and all the seasoning has fallen to the bottom of the bag.

So, again the simple seasoned potato chip and the world of science collide. To ensure that seasoning sticks, Golden Flake and other chip makers have to understand why seasoning sticks.

Enter the scientists

Quote: I have no special talents, I am only passionately curious.

– *Albert Einstein*

Enter the scientists. Scientists at Ohio State, heck – it's a long winter and your football team has been folding like a cheap card table, so you might as well so something with your time – scientists at Ohio State examined a number of factors that determine how salt adheres to potato chips.

And there is not just one factor. Again, the numbers of factors involved make you realize what a small miracle it is that we even have barbecue chips. But thank God we do!

The factors that make seasoning stick to a chip include surface oil content (SOC), chip temperature, the time between frying and coating the product, oil composition, salt particle size, salt crystal shape and the use of electrostatics.

Okay, this is more complicated than it looks.

But we can make it simple.

The scientists fried chips in soybean, olive, corn, peanut and coconut oils to study the effects of oil composition. They non-electrostatically coated NaCl (salt) crystals of five different particle sizes and three different shapes onto the chips. Using a powder applicator, five different sizes of salt were electrostatically applied onto all SOC chips. A feeder, which simulates a moving conveyor belt used in commercial settings, removed the salt.

Now before you buy another bag of chips, I want you to memorize the above paragraph, stand in the potato chip aisle and impress the other shoppers with your knowledge. Of course, if you even have a semblance of a life, this would be a bad idea.

Regarding seasoning, I lied – that wasn't simple. What it really means is that scientists tested a bunch of salt crystals on a bunch of chips and found that the main factor in making seasoning stick to a chip is surface oil content (SOC).

The chips with the highest SOC had the highest adhesion of salt, making SOC the most dominant factor. And the hotter the chip is when it comes out of the fryer, the better the seasoning sticks.

So seasoning sticks best to hot, oily chips. I know, I know – it took government research money *to figure that out?* It does make one wonder.

Okay, we are done with our seasoning lesson.

Whoops, maybe not.

You do not want large chunks of seasoning for chips. You want small particles. The scientists found that increasing the size of the salt particles decreased the extent of adhesion on all SOC chips. In other words, the small particles of salt stuck better to the surface of the chips.

But of course, even in the world of chips and seasoning, you are not going to make everybody happy.

Every now and then, a few missteps

Quote: Never interrupt your enemy when he is making a mistake.

– *Napoleon Bonaparte*

You can pick the wrong seasoning for your chips.

Jim Beam introduced potato chips that taste like bourbon. There is no actual alcohol in the chips, but parents were outraged, as this appeared to be introducing the Jim Beam brand and the concept of alcohol to children at an early age.

In fact the parents were so upset, that when they got home, they set the kids in front of the television, where the average child sees 8,000 murders before graduating from elementary school, and the parents had a drink. Or two.

Okay, I made that part up.

But Jim Beam did think that bourbon flavored potato chips were a good idea. Note that you do not see them on the market anymore.

Golden Flake is also not perfect. It once chose caffeine seasoning for a line of chips.

Whoops.

Here is part of a news story explaining the logic behind this 'caffeine seasoning'.

For a generation already buzzing on energy drinks, here's a new snack – potato chips coated with caffeine. NRG Phoenix Fury Potato Chips taste like extra-spicy barbecue chips, but they come with a caution label: not recommended for pregnant or nursing women, young children or anyone who is sensitive to caffeine.

The largest bag of Phoenix Fury chips weighs 3½ ounces, and the chip maker says downing the whole thing would be the caffeine equivalent of drinking 3½ big cups of brewed coffee. The chips won't yellow your teeth like a mug of Colombian, but they will turn your fingertips bright orange… "Energy drinks are the No. 1 growth item in convenience stores and supermarkets. As we looked at it, the people buying those are the same customers we have," said Golden Flake spokeswoman Julie McLaughlin.

Needless to say, caffeine flavored chips were not one of Golden Flake's marketing highlights, and the reasons will be explored even further in the Marketing section of this book.

Back to Seasoning

But the seasoning on your potato chip didn't just happen. Someone, somewhere took a bunch of chemicals and played around with them, trying to get that one flavor that was over the top, that would make consumers beg for a bag of chips. One 'over the top flavor' that worked well for Golden Flake were Sweet Heat chips.

I am not being facetious when I say a "bunch of chemicals". Flavors are created by blending tiny amounts of chemicals. In fact, some flavorists, yes there are really flavorists, often compare their work with composing music. And that actually is not a bad analogy. Do you want a heavy metal flavoring on your chips that will blow the customer away? Do you want a Latin Tango of a flavor, hot and spicy? Or do you want a classical music flavor, soft, soothing, but tasty?

A single compound often supplies the dominant aroma. Amyl acetate, for example, is 'the dominant note' of banana flavor. When distilled from bananas with a solvent, it's defined as natural. When produced by mixing vinegar with amyl alcohol, adding sulfuric acid as a catalyst, it's defined as artificial. But it's the same flavor, making you wonder how much difference there really is between natural and artificial ingredients.

But no matter how you get the banana flavor, both artificial and natural flavors are made at the same chemical plants.

The Real World of Golden Flake

We will go through an 80-pound bag of salt in about 45 minutes. Your chip is going to be 1.1 to 1.4% salt, so if you are doing 32 hundred pounds an hour of potato chips which are going to use a lot more salt than a tortilla chip. You only do about 13 hundred pounds of tortilla chips an hour and they are about 1% salt.

We have three different suppliers, it is not table salt, it's flake salt that stays on there when the chip is done.

And you have to use different grinds of salt. It is a flake of salt ground very small for a potato chip – with the pretzel they have a huge flake.

– *David Jones*

Little things add up

This morning I walked into the door and we are talking about a seasoning and a particular yeast that is becoming unavailable.

We talk about a particular seasoning that is not being made anymore and how is that going to affect ingredients. Taro yeast is made by two companies in the US. Sure, some companies outside the US make the yeast, but as far as a certified food ingredient, only two companies make it in the US.

One taro yeast is made off wood-based pulp; they grind wood into pulp and they grow the yeast off of moistened wood pulp, then they harvest the yeast and it gives you a flavor profile when added to certain other ingredients and it gives a certain type of flavor.

The other taro yeast is manufactured from ground-up sugar cane pieces, which are then moistened and the yeast grows on that. That yeast gives you a different flavor than the one off of the wood pulp.

The company that is making the yeast off the sugar cane is the one that is no longer going to be able to provide it to us and there is a difference in taro yeast flavor and we are trying to come up with a way to make sure that our consumer does not pick up a difference in flavor.

We try to be as consistent as we can, and the last thing we

want is to get letters from our consumers saying, "Why the heck did you change?"

That happens because our consumers are pretty dedicated and pretty loyal and they can go out and buy the Evil Empires' chips at any place at any price. Frito-Lay has seasonings that may be similar to ours but our flavoring is really derived in different ways that appeal to people in the Southeast states.

Do you can see that a little thing like a yeast not being available can turn into a big thing?

For instance, our barbecue chip is a special barbecue and we gear it towards our niche market of Southern tastes. Big companies have to appeal to a nationwide audience, but we have one group that we need to appeal to. We have a lot of people that go in the store, and we don't have as many square feet on the gondola, but our loyal customers will go hunt Sweet Heat potato chips down, they will go hunt down Dill potato chips, because they know they really like the flavor.

So it is very important for Golden Flake to be consistent in flavor. It makes a big difference; we test a lot of flavors and we want to be consistent in flavors and my main job every day and also our COO's, is just asking questions.

You learn a lot by asking questions.

– *David Jones*

Reality

By the way, we are not a bad salt contributor. The reason people say salty snacks, all the salt is typically on the surface and you get the salt sensation immediately. So it tastes salty, but we don't have near enough salt as a lot of products – a lot of canned vegetables – because ours is all on the surface.

– *Wayne Pate*

Chapter 4

Packaging

A lot of times when a package says "Open Other End", I purposely open the end where it says that.
– George Carlin

Introduction: Well we have visited the world of potato farms, storage, production, seasoning, cardboard boxes and these are a very small part of this thing we call business. We have seen how one invention builds upon another and how one coincidence leads to another coincidence and suddenly, you have a $6 billion dollar business hiring thousands of people. But by this point, you should be developing an appreciation of how a simple product, like a potato chip, is like a 1,000 piece jigsaw puzzle. It takes a lot of pieces, all carefully coordinated, to bring chips to market. And just when you think the puzzle is completed, up pops another piece, called packaging.

North American corporations spend $50 billion to $100 billion annually on packaging, and they all want to spend less.

When you look at any bag of Golden Flake potato chips, you are looking at a modern marvel.

I am not talking about the chips inside the bag, but the bag itself.

Golden Flake is not only in the transportation business and the water and sewer business, but it is also in the packaging business.

An intent of this book is to make you realize that nothing in business is simple. Even potato chip packaging.

What makes a good package?

Actually and this will come as no surprise to you – several things.

First it has to sell the product. It has to have graphics that the consumer recognizes and wants to buy.

There is no salesman in the store, telling you to buy the product. The bag and the right graphics have to do the selling.

A potato chip bag has to protect the product. And there must be compatibility between the chip and the plastic packaging material. That means the chips cannot absorb any of the chemicals from the plastic or else the consumer is getting more than he bargained for in that chip. Some salt, some grease and oh yes – a little dose of chemicals.

The package also determines the shelf life of the chip. How many days, after it leaves the Golden Flake factory, can you eat the chip? That is why every bag carries an expiration date.

But think about this. You could make a super-duper package that could give the chip a shelf life of two months. Heck that will make the sales manager happy – he has two months to sell the chips. If the shelf life of the chip is reduced to eight days, he has to sell the chips within eight days.

But lesser shelf life means reduced packaging costs.

With means that – sure you can make a package that will last for two years – and fill it with Golden Flake chips. But the package would be too expensive.

In addition to protecting the chips, a bag for chips must have mechanical strength. It cannot break when dropped; it should not tear or puncture.

A quick aside to show how tough potato chip bags are, several potato chips bags were dropped over Niagara Falls and not one bag broke open.

To make this packaging even more complicated, there is a relationship between packaging cost and the damage done to a product. How many broken chips can Golden Flake live with in every bag? Or should it build a bulletproof bag to protect every single chip. That of course would, again, be too expensive.

Cost-Benefit Analysis or Is it really worth the time and effort.

Here is another great economics term – cost-benefit analysis. Cost-benefit really means, how much time and effort are you willing to put into something? Is it worth the money for the profit you will make? If you are in the counterfeiting business, why would you waste your time counterfeiting cans of Campbell's tomato soup. If you are going to counterfeit something, counterfeit Viagra. Time better spent and a much bigger profit. Of course, according to my lawyer, this paragraph never existed.

Cost-benefit analysis also extends to potato chip packaging. Engineers actually consider different alternatives between the packaging cost and the percentage of broken chips. They actually do laboratory simulation, have a monkey throw the chips, packaged in different packages, against the wall, then they open the bag and check how many chips were broken.

Hang in there and we will talk about cost-benefit further down the line.

Okay, I made the part about the monkey up. But the engineers plot graphs and do all kinds of scientific stuff to plot the total cost versus the percent of damage.

In other words, you can't protect every chip in the bag from breakage, but how many broken chips can you live with to reduce your cost of packaging.

By the way, an interesting aside about packaging. Do you notice that sometimes you have to use your teeth to open a potato chip bag? Well studies have shown that consumers rate the chips or any food product as 'fresher' if the bag is harder to open. Chips in a hard-to-open bag are literally viewed as tastier and crisper.

How many people does it take to 'build' a better potato chip bag?

That Golden Flake bag that protects your potato chips is actually a result of several industries working together.

Industries dealing with safety, shelf life, convenience, appearance, cost of raw materials, transportation costs, handling, law, manufacturing, equipment, and more all combine to make a 'simple potato chip' bag.

Wait, we can throw even more into the mix. Making that perfect package also includes marketing, art, graphics, psychology and law.

Whoa! What do all these people do?

Well, they hang around and drink a lot of beer.

Whoops, those are writers.

The people involved in packaging have real jobs.

The chemical engineer considers the chemistry of the food within the package and its reaction with the package material. The mechanical engineer worries about the machines to make the package. Physics and mathematics deal with size, shape, mass and structure of the package.

But you said law was also involved, as in lawyers.

Hmm – check the end of this chapter. This is just one federal regulation stating what Golden Flake can and cannot put in nutritional information. Which every bag must have. As well as an expiration date.

Hmm, what if you came with an expiration date?

"Don't buy that new truck, Ricky. You are expiring next year."

Hmm, which may be a reason to buy the new truck.

Anyway – in the real world of economics it is amazing how many industries it takes just to produce a simple Golden Flake bag.

How many bags are in a bag?

Actually there is only one bag. But it has at least three barriers.

Now, potato chips have three enemies. Light, water and oxygen. Actually hungry teenagers are also a threat, but let's move on.

One barrier protects the chips from absorbing moisture. As the food scientists like to say, which is probably why you don't meet many food scientists at fun parties, food scientists like to say, "A chip, like every food product, has optimum moisture content with respect to its stability."

In other words, no moisture in that bag. Because no one likes a soggy chip, so the package has to protect the chips from water. Leave a bag of chips open on a humid day and you will get soggy chips.

And, oh boy, I get to sound like a scientist here, you don't want 'oxidative rancidity of the snack'.

Okay, time for a short definition here. Potatoes are cooked in oil. When you cook a chip in oil, the oil replaces the water in the chip. Some chips can be about 80% oil.

The problem with oil is that oxygen and oil do not get along. When oxygen meets oil, oxidation takes place which means the chip can become very smelly and taste bad. It can become rancid.

That is why there is no oxygen in a bag of chips. Before they seal it up, they blast nitrogen into the bag which drives out the oxygen.

Another key word – photodegradation. No that is not what happens when you take a photo of me.

Light is bad for food. The exposure of food to light can result in its deterioration (also known as photodegradation).

Potato chips prepared by deep fat frying in oil are susceptible to photodegradation and develop off-odors and off-flavors on exposure to light.

Off-odors and off-flavors. That means that they start to smell and taste bad.

That's why potato chip bags have a barrier that light can't get through. And that is why the bag is opaque. You can shine a flashlight on a bag of chips and that light will not reach the chips inside. Whereas you can sign a light in my ears and my eyes will light up.

Another barrier must be established against oil or grease – we don't want oily spots on the outside of the bag. And there is a fine science in creating these barriers. The type of thickness and coating for each barrier is scientifically established.

These barriers are just the inside of the bag. You still have to glue a printed film to the outside of the bag. That printed film is what you see when you buy a bag of chips. It says Golden Flake and has the logos and the nutritional requirements and all that fun stuff that makes you want to pick up the bag and take it home.

And of course, opening a potato chip bag can be tough to do. The long seam in the back of the bag must be strong so the bag doesn't split when it is loaded onto a truck, taken off the truck, placed on a store shelf, picked up by a shopper, thrown into a shopping cart, then thrown into the shopper's car and then thrown onto a shelf in the kitchen. But you can open a bag of chips by leaving it in the bottom of a shopping cart and accidently dropping a gallon of milk on it; something, I am embarrassed to say, I have done more than once.

In short, you need barriers in every bag of chips. So the texture, flavor and aroma will be like the very day they placed the chips in the bag. The goal is that a Golden Flake chip will taste just as fresh as the day it came off the conveyor belt. This flavor must be preserved through storage of the chips, transportation of the chips and when the customer opens the bag.

An oxymoron: Metalized Plastic? Or Look Out – More Science Ahead

As we have just discussed, every Golden Chip bag is multi-layered. The pigmented plastic films prevent light from entering. Metalized films are barriers to gases and light.

Metalized films?

Yes, one layer of the Golden Flake bag is made of 'metalized film'.

That means scientists have designed a barrier in a potato chip bag that is part metal and part plastic. It was designed to keep light out.

Which is really kind of cool, but how do they do it?

To metalize a plastic like PP or PET, the aluminum is put in a chamber at a temperature of 1500–1800°C. The aluminum vaporizes into tiny particles that stick to the plastic film.

I know – sounds like science fiction. Where else can you use cool terms like "vaporize"?

It gets even cooler. Look out for the vacuum tube!

No air molecules can be present when the aluminum is vaporized. The air molecules would deflect the aluminum. So the whole process is done in a vacuum chamber.

Plus oxygen would cause the aluminum to be dull. Which would be bad, as you need a highly reflective shiny aluminum on the plastic to reflect light away from the chips in the bag.

And, getting back to costs, as we always must in economics, it is much cheaper for the manufacturer to metalize a film rather than use a thin layer of aluminum foil in the package.

Paper or plastic?

A criticism of many plastic products, including the bags that Golden Flake uses, is that they are not biodegradable, like you and I are.

But as in every argument surrounding the environment and business, there are always two ways of looking at the environmental challenge.

Golden Flake could go back to paper packaging. Except that paper can't provide moisture, light, and gas barriers. And, again, these barriers are needed to keep the chips fresh.

Also consider this. Replacement of plastics by traditional packages would double the volume of packaging waste and quadruple the weight.

Why your potato chip bag shrinks in the microwave

If you are sitting around one night, totally bored, you can always play "Shrink the Bag in the Microwave". Hmm, of course you could always rent a DVD, which might be even more fun. The plot would have to be better than watching a bag shrink.

But, there is a reason for the game. It helps you to understand the science behind a potato chip bag. In fact potato chip bags shrink in the microwave because of the material that the potato chip bag is made of.

When Golden Flake selects a material to package their products in, they look for a material that is relatively lightweight (they are selling chips, not bags, and shipping costs money), a material that can keep out oxygen and moisture and one that is easy to work with in high-speed packaging machines.

It also has to be able to leap tall buildings in a single bound.

Okay, maybe not, but as you have seen, a lot is expected from any bag.

Okay, tongue-twister time.

Polymer resins such as polyethylene terephthalate (PET) fit these requirements well. When melted and squeezed under high pressure into thin sheets (sometimes as thin as 5 microns), these plastics make the thin, flexible, air-proof, heat-workable, super package that Golden Flake requires.

Golden Flake graphics are printed onto the material while it is in its flat, continuous sheet format. Rolls of the material are then sent to the Golden Flake factory, fed into high-speed packaging machines that fold the material together, and heat-seal it, then cut the material into individual bags to be filled with chips before again being heat-sealed.

We can play "Shrink the Bag" because the bags are heat-sealed.

Polymers are long chains of molecules and the natural form of a polymer is to curl up. The high-pressure squeezing at the bag factory stretches the polymer chains out to strong, thin sheets. This high pressure squeezing locks the chains in their stretched form.

However, heat up the Golden Flake bag in the microwave and the chains break free and try to return to their natural curled-up state – the bag is 'shrinking'.

As the chains shrink, they are still bound to each other, and still stacked together in the thin layers that make up the bag, so the bag retains the same shape, only smaller.

Code Chip or Fun with Acronyms

Quote: Brb, ttyl ok? Wow, I saved a 'ton' of time with those acronyms.

– Stephen Colbert

The famous acronym NAICS (North American Industrial Classification System) has been used since 1997 by all the statistical agencies Uncle Sam employs.

It replaced the 1987 acronym 'SIC' (Standard Industrial Classification) code, developed in the 1930s.

Why do we even need these codes?

First it makes the IRS happy. More about that later.

Also it makes researchers happy. All the government, state agencies, trade associations, researchers and other statistical organizations use the data generated by these codes to predict economic trends and analyze historical patterns.

With NAICS all the businesses that use similar processes to produce goods or services are grouped together. NAICS covers 1170 industries and a six-digit code identifies each industry.

Here is how they designed the old SIC code for potato chips and how they designed the new NAICS code for potato chips.

POTATO CHIPS a la SIC

20 Food and Kindred Products
209 Miscellaneous Food Preparations and Kindred Products
2096 Potato Chips, Corn Chips and Similar Snacks

POTATO CHIPS a la NAICS

31 Manufacturing
311 Food Manufacturing
3119 Other Food Manufacturing
31191 Snack Food Manufacturing
311919 Other Snack Food Manufacturing

So if you make potato chips, your old SIC code was 2096 but your new NAICS code is 311919. The government likes to add as many numbers as possible.

Enter the IRS. They are always lurking somewhere!

The IRS uses these codes to screen Golden Flake's tax return against others with the same code. This will tell the IRS if Golden Flake's income and expenses are in line with industry norms. If they're not, Golden Flake can expect an audit.

The Real World of Golden Flake
How the price of oil affects packaging or the economics of packaging...

The resins that are used to make our bags are made from oil.

Packaging film is a plastic and plastics are derived from oil, and when the price of oil goes up the price of plastics goes up, and the price of resins that make our packaging film goes up.

Packaging film is very price sensitive because there are only so many resin-producing refineries in this country. Most of them are located down in Texas and Louisiana. They make gasoline in petroleum refineries and oil and things. But the leftover products, after all these things are made, are used to make resins.

And they turn these resins into packaging film.

They make the resins into those little pellets and they sell those pellets on the open market to packaging film companies. The packaging film companies then melt the resin and laminate the packaging film which turns into the Golden Flake bag.

And when we have hurricanes in summer those refineries are shut down. When a hurricane shuts down a refinery, we can expect the packaging film companies to start coming to us almost immediately.

"Oh the price of resin is way up, we might have to have a price increase and you know the refineries were down for three weeks and we heard some rumblings that they were going to raise prices and they have. And as the price of oil has gone up the past few years we have taken price increases in packaging film costs..."

We know what they are going to tell us. We try not to be too dependent on just one packaging film supplier. We have at any one time up to four suppliers that supply us and we kind of played one group off another.

If Group A says we are going to have to raise the price on your packaging film per impression, and we haven't heard from the other packaging companies, we will say, "Look, your competitors have not raised the prices and if you want to raise them, fine but we will have to look at a readjustment on business..."

So you can't just have one supplier you're beholden to; you try to have multiple, in order to go ahead and play one against the other in order to keep your prices stable and as low as possible.

Every few years we go through a bidding process, we have so much packaging film on every item we run, from a five ounce bag of potato chips which is a huge run, down to an item that we may only run once a week.

So we put all the packaging film out for bid and then we let the packaging film companies secret bid and then we look at the bids and then reward the contracts to the packaging film company that comes in with the best price.

That is the way we manage packaging film, to try to keep it competitive. So far we have been keeping our prices stable.
— *David Jones*

Packaging. Bag it please...

Get your bag too thin when the bags get handled, when they get to the store, when they get to the shelf, too thin of a bag will looked crinkled. It will have poor shelf appearance. You have to have a certain stiffness in the packaging film to make that bag look good.

There are a couple of things, technology-wise, that we look for in packaging film. We worry about how that actual packaging is put together. Is the oxygen outside that bag migrating inside that bag? We want to keep the outside atmosphere from the inside of our bag because that causes our chips to oxidize.

And when the bag boy puts a bag by a Tide detergent, you don't want to get home and have your chips tasting like Tide detergent.

So we go ahead and look at the barriers to keep things out, then we look and try to see what we want inside that bag.

What do we want inside that bag when we dump the finished product in the bag? We gas flush the bag with nitrogen; nitrogen is heavier than air, so you go ahead and put a blast of nitrogen down the packaging tube as that bag is being made, and that nitrogen pushes the air out.

The air goes out and the nitrogen stays in and the bag is sealed up. The nitrogen keeps oxidation down to a minimum level while that bag is waiting to be sold.

30 years ago you bought a bag of chips, it had air inside

and the oxidation process took place much quicker. That meant we only have a limited amount of time to sell that bag before the air oxidizes the oil inside the bag. Potato chips are basically 70% oil.

The bags we package our chips in now, the technology has been developed over the past 30 years. We have found ways to keep out the air and we found out ways to keep the nitrogen in. But the oxygen always wants to get back in and the nitrogen always wants to get out, so you have to have barriers both ways. In fact, it's only been the past five years where we have gotten to the point where we have pretty good packaging film.

Many people take the Golden Flake bag for granted, but we have tested off and on different packaging films. One was even called the tin can, because nothing escaped from it, but the cost was too high. There is always a balance between cost and perfection. How perfect does that bag have to be to satisfy the consumer, keep the product fresh and not cost us an arm and a leg?

Our best test, remember heat and light are the worst enemies of our snack food, so the best test for us, and this sounds simple, put the product in an aluminum route truck or the trunk of a car and stick it out in the parking lot in a Birmingham hot, humid summer. It is a great test.

If it can survive that, we set our shelf life, the expiration date for our chips for the absolute worse conditions, so that the consumer will never put a bag in those conditions. Even though you were going to put that product past the expiration date in a lighted pantry at a high temperature, that bag would last a month or so after that expiration date.

We test our bags in the worse conditions, so that if you put it in the hat rack of your car in the summertime and it is sitting back there with terrible elements every day we want it to still taste good when you open that bag.

Is there some money involved in that? Yes, maybe we could cut our sales expenses another half of a percent if we extended the shelf life.

When it comes to the product and the packaging, it really gets down to one basic question: "Would I eat this?"

The last step in quality control is that route person who is putting that bag on the shelf, who nods his head and says, "Yes, I would buy this; yes, I would eat this."

If not, don't put it on the shelf.

– *Mark McCutcheon*

Say What?

We promised we would show you a quick list of some of the food labeling regulations that Golden Flake must follow. Again –and this is a basic lesson in economics – you are never alone when producing a product. The government is always your partner. Here is just part – the list goes on and on – and I couldn't torture you that much, but here is just part of the federal requirements for labeling potato chips – there are over 100 sections in the entire document:

(e)(1) Because the use of a "free" or "low" claim before the name of a food implies that the food differs from other foods of the same type by virtue of its having a lower amount of the nutrient, only foods that have been specially processed, altered, formulated, or reformulated so as to lower the amount of the nutrient in the food, remove the nutrient from the food, or not include the nutrient in the food, may bear such a claim (e.g. "low sodium potato chips").

(2) Any claim for the absence of a nutrient in a food, or that a food is low in a nutrient when the food has not been specially processed, altered, formulated, or reformulated to qualify for that claim shall indicate that the food inherently meets the criteria and shall clearly refer to all foods of that type and not merely to the particular brand to which the labeling attaches (e.g.

"corn oil, a sodium-free food").

(f) A nutrient content claim shall be in type size no larger than two times the statement of identity and shall not be unduly prominent in type style compared to the statement of identity.

(2) The use of the statement on the food implicitly characterizes the level of the nutrient in the food and is not consistent with such a definition, but the label carries a disclaimer adjacent to the statement that the food is not "low" in or a "good source" of the nutrient, such as "only 200 mg sodium per serving, not a low sodium food." The disclaimer must be in easily legible print or type and in a size no less than that required by §101.105(i) for the net quantity of contents statement except where the size of the claim is less than two times the required size of the net quantity of contents statement, in which case the disclaimer shall be no less than one-half the size of the claim but no smaller than one-sixteenth of an inch unless the package complies with §101.2(c)(5), in which case the disclaimer may be in type of not less than one thirty-second of an inch, or...

(3) The statement does not in any way implicitly characterize the level of the nutrient in the food and it is not false or misleading in any respect (e.g. "100 calories" or "5 grams of fat"), in which case no disclaimer is required.

(4) "Percent fat free" claims are not authorized by this paragraph. Such claims shall comply with §101.62(b)(6).

(j) A food may bear a statement that compares the level of a nutrient in the food with the level of a nutrient in a reference food. These statements shall be known as "relative claims" and include "light", "reduced", "less" (or "fewer"), and "more" claims.

(i)(A) For "less" (or "fewer") and "more" claims, the reference food may be a dissimilar food within a product category that can generally be substituted for one another in the diet (e.g. potato chips as reference for pretzels, orange juice as a reference for vitamin C tablets) or a similar food (e.g. potato chips as reference for potato chips, one brand of multivitamin as reference for another brand of multivitamin).

Chapter 5

Transportation: Just throw it in the truck.
Hmm – bad idea

When Edward Gibbon was writing about the fall of the Roman Empire in the late 18th century, he could argue that transportation hadn't changed since ancient times. An imperial messenger on the Roman roads could get from Rome to London even faster in AD 100 than in 1750. But by 1850, and even more obviously today, all of that has changed.
– Walter Meade

Introduction: We hope that by now, from raw materials to the sophisticated chip bags, you are getting the inkling that businesses deal with a lot ('a lot' is a technical term used by sophisticated business writers) just to get those chips to market. And you are learning, chapter by chapter, how much it takes to understand business. Now – and pardon the pun – let's hit the road to further develop your understanding of business.

Golden Flake is not only in the snack food business. It is in the transportation business.

And that means you think how to maximize the load in your trucks. Fuel is too expensive to waste carrying half a load.

Yet, many companies do carry half a load.

Here's why. Truck loading is a trade off between weight, volume, balance and compactness. US law limits the gross vehicle weight of a tractor, trailer and its cargo to 80,000 pounds when traveling on the interstate highway system. Federal and state safety regulations further restrict how big the trailers and tractor-trailer combinations can be.

For example, the length of a trailer can only be 53 feet; the length of tandem trailers can only be 28 feet.

As you are beginning to see, you can't just toss stuff in the truck and head out. As this book emphasizes time and time again, every phase of business involves layer upon layer of complexity.

For instance there are restrictions on the way you position the cargo weight in the truck. No axle is allowed to bear more than 34,000 pounds. And that is bad news because your load can reach one legal maximum before the truck is even full. Your truck 'weighs out', for example, before it 'cubes out'. That is why many manufacturers, including Golden Flake, have developed rules of thumb that help them load trucks as full as possible without paying fines for overloading trucks.

A brewer, for example, may limit its truckloads to 44,000 pounds of beer, because the weight of the tractor, trailer and 'tonnage' (pallets and packing material) will take up 36,000 pounds of the 80,000-pound limit.

But this 'full' truckload is not really a truckload. It is half-empty. It only contains 22 pallets of beer, each weighing about 2,000 lbs, stacked five feet high in the trailer. There still is 4 feet of empty space from the front of the trailer to the tailgate.

Whoops.

So how do you change that?

Well, truck loading is really a game of Tetris.

If the brewer also delivers corn chips, boxed and stacked in 4-foot high, 1,000-lb pallets, it could replace 11 pallets of beer on a truck with 22 pallets of corn chips. Plus, by mixing this light and heavy freight on each truck, the beer and snack food manufacturer could deliver 44 pallets of potato chips (a full truckload) and 22 pallets of beer (two full truckloads) in two trucks.

But the question becomes –"Why use pallets?" They cost your extra weight. Look inside any Golden Flake truck and the boxers are stacked on top of each other with no pallets.

And Golden Flake realizes that it is good to ask for help now and then, because so much money is invested in transporting chips across the Southeast.

So they use a computer program designed by UPS which helps Golden Flake maximize every load.

How clever is UPS in figuring out how to save money delivering anything?

This is the same company that favors right-hand turns where possible, again to reduce running time. The less time trucks spend sitting in left-turn lanes, the less fuel they burn. This simple move saves UPS $600 million a year.

Let's detour the truck to understand some basic terms or some real cool economics terms you can impress your friends with

Quote: Competition is the keen cutting edge of business, always shaving away at costs.

– *Henry Ford*

Let's take a quick detour to learn some key economics terms: fixed costs, consistent variable costs and load-specific-costs.

Fixed costs and consistent variable costs apply to every aspect of manufacturing, but for no apparent reason, I thought I would explain them here.

Just kidding. Using a truck as an example is a very good way to understand fixed and variable costs.

Fixed Costs: every expense your operation pays if all your trucks were parked for a month. Items like truck payments, office expenses (including your paycheck), insurance, licenses, taxes… These are figured annually and divided by 365 days = Fixed Cost per Day.

Consistent Variable Costs: are the expenses which occur every time your trucks are rolling. Items like: tires, repairs, maintenance, washes, parts, etc.

Load-Specific Costs: any expense which changes load-by-load or trip by trip. Items include: fuel, tolls, labor and, if paid by the mile, your driver's pay. These are amounts on a load-by-load basis, and figured as a single dollar figure (Your Load Specific Cost).

And a little trivia. This time I must admit it is for no apparent reason except it ties into shipping potatoes. The trailers that carry the potatoes generally have a refrigeration system that keep the temperature around 42 degrees.

The Real World of Golden Flake
Transportation thoughts

When you are in the potato chip business you have to be in the transportation business. You have to know how to efficiently run your fleet. You need efficient engines, efficient space to haul the maximum amount and we have done all those things.

We were a pioneer in studying windscreens on these great big trucks, we can improve fuel efficiency by deflecting the wind over those big trailers so you don't have a headwind pushing against you all the time.

We have learned to haul product all the way into Texas and make it pay, because of the efficiency of our trucks and our tractors and because we have the largest, widest, tallest trucks you can run on the road. And we fill them front to back, top to bottom and have efficient engines pulling them and therefore we can go further than a lot of people can.

Because of fuel costs and because you want to maintain freshness and quality in your product, you can only haul so far. We can haul further out than we used to, but you obviously need plants, conveniently located, so you can haul finished products. So that limits how far you can go without building plants.

We started in Birmingham in 1923 and we moved out by what we called the 'ink blotter' method. You drop a drop of ink on a blotter and it sort of spreads out. We never wanted to jump territories; we wanted to grow from the South.

Another thing in growing is typically you want to sell everybody, you want to sell up and down the street, mom and pop stores, convenience stores and you also want to sell chains. When you sell a chain, a chain does not want you to serve only part of the stores. They want you to serve all the stores, so their stores will be the same. Therefore when you sell a chain, you have to be able to supply where that chain is located.

We have seen companies bite off more than they can chew. And so we try to grow very systemically. Going into a new market is extremely expensive. It takes time, sometimes even years before you can make a profit, before you can grow enough critical mass. You don't want to be one-inch thick over 10,000 square miles. You want to be 15 inches thick over a few square miles.

So we have stuck to the South. We are a Southern company and if we wanted to move up North, we could, but because of the logistics we pretty much stuck to the South. And because of that, because our focus is the South, we can say that we were the original Southern potato chip; we are one year older than Frito-Lay.

Transportation advice

All our trucks are floor stacked; we do not use pallets. Why add extra weight to the load? The truck is actually stacked from floor to ceiling. We have to and will use every inch of that truck, as fuel is too expensive!

You just don't put 700 cases on a truck. If the truck is going from Birmingham to Decatur to Huntsville then Nashville – you have to load the truck that way – Nashville goes in first, then Huntsville, then Decatur, so when your first stop is Decatur, you can just pull the cases off. Every packing of a truck has to be planned to the last detail.

We have 328 routes, we have 55 distributors that represent

another 100 routes – so we are pushing the 450 route range for the Golden Flake product across the Southeast.

And it varies from route to route; we have to deliver to some supermarkets three days a week, some supermarkets we have to deliver to seven times a week and some convenience stores two times a week, some once a week. A rule of thumb is two times a week for C-stores and three times a week for grocery stores.

–*Randy Bates*

Keep on Trucking

Three years ago we were planning for five dollar gas for our vehicles. You have to keep asking questions. And we have to ask, if gas reaches five dollars a gallon what are we going to do? Well we have this many routes times this many trucks times this much fuel, so that is going to increase this much %, and we just can't do that.

A little investment in technology in our route trucks helped us. For example we purchased a road net system from UPS. We can go in and GPS every stop. With this information, a good manager can route trucks the best way, so you are not on a route and have a $2,000 dollar route average and I am over here on this route and have a $12,000 average.

So we have some parameters, how do we hit all the spots we need to hit this many times a week and do that efficiently and cut our mileage?

Well to cut delivery costs, in Birmingham, we placed three warehouses around the city. So all the route drivers and the trucks don't have to come to our main plant like they used to. We put the warehouses in different areas of the city; the drivers were closer to their stops and their homes. We sold one of those warehouses because we didn't need three, we only needed two and it maps out pretty well; we save 16% in mileage just in Birmingham.

– Mark McCutcheon

Shorten the distance

Now we typically have not gone on up the valley towards Canada, the Winnipeg area. But we have established relationships with growers that far north, because in a bad season, you need potatoes.

Optimally we would love to buy more Wisconsin, Indiana potatoes because it is a shorter distance for the freight to Birmingham. So we use the markets; we take the closest market we can buy potatoes so we can ship to the plant. Because the freight can be ridiculous.

Getting the potatoes on the truck down to Birmingham can be a science in itself. In the summertime, you can roll those trucks pretty rapidly. So you dig them, load them, open the vents in the truck so you don't suffocate the potatoes and so air blows through them and typically that works fine and nothing changes in the potato.

In the spring, we are cooking them right away; we are not putting them in the warehouse. We are digging, and cooking. And pretty much we get the trucks to flow in as needed. It's our 'just in time' inventory system.

So we buy them to chip on arrival. What you want is a chipping potato that cooks well. We take samples when the potatoes arrive. We put a hole in some potatoes and put them through the fryer and we can check the potato with the hole in it and see how it fried.

– Wayne Pate

Loading the trucks

The shipping department gets sheets that tell what goes to each route guy, and they load the boxes on the trucks.

Each driver will see about 786 boxes of chips. One truck might have five routes on it, each one of these routes has ordered the items packed on the truck. If this truck is going from here to Decatur to Huntsville then Nashville, then they have to load Nashville, Huntsville, Decatur so when they get to Decatur, they don't have to unload 700 cases, and put them back on, because they packed the truck the wrong way. On a truck it has to be planned out to the last detail.

– *Julie McLaughlin*

Chapter 6

Marketing Concepts: You Do It So Well

Marketing takes a day to learn. Unfortunately it takes a lifetime to master.

– Phil Kotler

Introduction: Okay, we have covered getting the potatoes to the plant, storing the potatoes, making the chips, the complex science behind making chips, the complex science behind a chip package, and we have even covered how you have to load trucks to minimize costs and maximize profit. But now we have to get people to buy our chips. Welcome to Marketing.

To survive as a small company in a snack food industry dominated by two giants Kraft and Frito-Lay, Golden Flake must clearly define its territory and use innovative marketing techniques to maintain and attract customers. Including, playing off of its brand name. To fully understand business, you need to understand marketing and the key role it plays in generating revenue for any company.

Frito-Lay dominates the salty snack foods industry (a fancy term for potato chips and salty snacks). Frito-Lay controls 67% of the market with total retail sales of about $45 billion a year. Kraft Foods, with the Nabisco brand business, holds second place with yearly retail sales of $29.7 billion. Compare these numbers to Golden Flake which has retail sales of about $114 million a year.

You could claim the industry has some elements of a monopoly as it is dominated by two large players. But Golden Flake hangs in there and so do other small regional manufacturers. They keep the business highly competitive.

How do they compete with the 'big boys'?

First, Golden Flake clearly defines its market to 12 Southern states. Then it markets extensively to that region.

Golden Flake flat-out understands where it sells chips.

More than 40% of all purchases of Golden Flake chips were made in supermarkets, food stores that reported annual sales of at least $2 million. Grocery stores, food stores with sales of less than $2 million annually, accounted for between 10 and 20% of Golden Flake.

The remaining chips were sold in convenience stores, mass merchandisers, and large general merchandise stores that also carried grocery items such as warehouse club stores, drugstores, vending machines, and other retail outlets such as delicatessens, liquor stores, and sports stadiums.

And Golden Flake understands the demand for potato chips is the highest at age 42. It's not as if there is a bunch of 42 year olds eating potato chips. They are buying the chips for their children. When the parent is 42, the average aged child of that parent is 14.

That may be a small point, but you have to understand who you are marketing to.

To compete for market share, here some key marketing strategies that Golden Flake uses:

- Communicate a market position that makes them different. Golden Flake is proud of being the "Crispiest Chip in the South".
- Start with a powerful brand mark since the brand is the focal point of the package. The consumer looks for brands he trusts. Be wary of changing your package. A brand should generally be in standard colors, such as blue, red, and yellow.
- Sell to your segment by knowing your consumer and speaking directly to him or her.
- Understand the category, the competitive matrix and the category norms. Study the competition for layout, type, color, style, product presentation nomenclature, saturation

and configuration.

- Design for shelf impact since the average shopper spends one to two seconds looking at the choices. The package must pop out.
- Sports Marketing Works – Golden Flake is a sponsor of the SEC, Talladega 500, the Sun Belt Conference, College Football Bowls, and all   local Southern universities.
- Get involved in the community.

I am not leaving you hanging here. All the above marketing criteria will be discussed in detail in the following section, where we enter *The Real World of Golden Flake*.

And sometimes a quote is so good, so concisely sums up a marketing philosophy that it should be heard twice. Here is such a quote:

We have done a terrific job of making sure Golden Flake is thought of and regarded highly. Our brand is our identity and our most powerful sales tool. We protect it and we work very hard at projecting a positive image day in and day out, with every employee, with all our tractors and trailers. We own our transportation system, we own over 320 trucks, but on the company's owned trucks we are very particular about presenting a very clean, neat image, trucks washed, to project the good food and our brand name.

– Randy Bates

One more tidbit before we head onto The Real World of Golden Flake.

You have to love the innovative ways a 'small company', like Golden Flake uses guerilla marketing. They cannot compete with the big boys when it comes to advertising spending, so they do great promotions within their Southern territory.

Here is an example of one such promotion:

Golden Flake Coach for A-Day

Register to win a chance to be an Honorary Coach at Golden Flake A-Day on Saturday, April 14th at Bryant-Denny Stadium!

One lucky Alabama football fan will be selected to serve as an honorary coach for the team's annual intrasquad game to close spring practice. The winner will receive:

- Spend half of the game in the team bench area
- Spend half of the game in the radio booth/press box area
- Coaching Gear to wear throughout the game
- Two (2) passes to the Tide Pride Luncheon
- Opportunity to call a play from the team playlist
- Official Alabama autographed ball
- Golden Flake prize pack
- Interview on CTSN radio broadcast

The Real World of Golden Flake
The importance of appearance or "Not a con job."

We have learned that color does make a difference. The biggest customer for our tortilla chip with green powder on it is the Texas prison system. They're our captive audience and they are the only ones who will eat it. No one likes the green color.

We have taste tested it three times and people refused to eat it, but once they tasted it they loved it.

But the prisoners had to taste it and they loved it – they are our biggest fans.

We are trying to roll it out to the general market without it being green – it looks like it's moldy or something, it looks horrible. I have taken it three different times and people won't touch it. You have to grovel and beg and no one will even taste it and then, when they do, they will eat the whole bag.

But you can't force people to eat it in a grocery store.

– *Julie McLaughlin, marketing director*

Advertising

Another important part of the sales equation is our marketing; marketing does a terrific job with the monies that we give them to spend. Unfortunately we don't have a big marketing budget, so we have to play to our consumers' strengths.

Those strengths are Southern taste, Southern football, Southern sports and we are not too worried about what other people say about us; we are worried about what our consumers say. In our Southern group of folks, we cover nine states – just the Southeast orientation. We have all grown up in this, so we know how to appeal to the folks that like our product and we know how to appeal to folks that come into the South, that's why we target Southern states and tastes.

So with the marketing campaign that we have, we combine that with a quality product, that plays a big portion, and finally to the service end of it as I alluded to earlier, we keep it clean and neat and healthy-looking on the shelf, and keep a full shelf, you got a winning combination that makes sense.

How little do we have to spend on advertising, next to our competitors like Frito-Lay? Well, they buy the Super Bowl as one of their spots and our annual budget would go to one Super Bowl spot. Yes, that would wipe out our annual advertising budget.

The Super Bowl is the most watched event, the premier advertising spot and our competitors run all kinds of spots. We don't try to run with them. There are carcasses of companies spread throughout the United States, who are not here anymore because they try to run with Frito-Lay.

You just don't try to run with Frito-Lay.

I am fond of saying: "A man has to know his limitations" and so we know our limitations, where to spend our money that generates the most bang for the buck.

You can't outspend Frito-Lay, so we have to depend on our

people being out there building that good will, from a management standpoint, not just the route level. And then we have to focus heavily on the marketing that we do have and try to appeal to the spectrum with the least amount of investment and we stretch it – we just can't spend with Frito-Lay, we don't even try.

The key parts of our marketing plan? Billboards play a big part in what we do today. The cost of TV is too much and it is too fragmented; you have over 100 cable channels and you don't know where to put your money, you don't have enough money to catch that broad spectrum. We have to be very selective and in today's environment TV is not a wise purchase for us.

We put spots on billboards throughout the Southeast that hit the biggest amount of cars going by and we have expanded that by a lot.

Our biggest expenditures are our sponsorships of athletics.

Sports marketing, we still have people referring to us as "Great Pair says The Bear." (After every Alabama football game Bear Bryant would sit at a desk which had a bag of Golden Flake chips on it, and discuss the game. This association proved so powerful that, even today, before Alabama football games, people lay bags of Golden Flake chips at the foot of the Bear Bryant statue.)

We get a lot of impact from that association and we get impact from our existing coaches as well. Sports marketing including the races at Talladega, most Southern college sports, that is where we get the biggest bang for our marketing dollars.

– *Randy Bates*

Marketing a new brand

How do you decide brand extension, market demand? We take a look at what is going on around us, we try to read up on journals, snack food association trends that are going on around the nation and then we try to apply them to our regional needs down here.

The best brand extension we have? We have a flavor in our potato chip line that is called Sweet Heat. Southerners love barbecue, whether it's tomato-based or vinegar-based, they just love barbecue. We have got a flavor that has a little heat to that barbecue. And it is a little sweet. So we call it Sweet Heat and it is our number one selling flavored potato chip.

And that took two years to roll out, tasting, tweaking, tweaking, tweaking. Once during testing, we took the Sweet Heat flavored chip to a test market and tried to limit within that market, or so we thought. Then we had people bootlegging it to other markets because we were selling so well in that market.

That was a successful rollout but it did cannibalize some of our other barbecue flavors – but it soon worked its way up to be our number one selling flavored potato chip. (Note, the concept of 'cannibalizing' is always on your mind when you consider introducing a new product. For instance, if you already have a best-selling barbecue chip, why introduce another one? Because the sales of a new flavored barbecue chip might take away market share from the original barbecue chip.)

Regarding research, we will tell the spice suppliers what flavor profile we are looking for and we will take the spices in here and our manufacturing people will apply it to X number bags of samples and we will pass them up and down the hall and let everyone taste them. They will answer yes, no or maybe. Then we will take the samples over to people in the plant and let them taste them, take it to the accounting department and let them taste them.

Now the financing department, you have to be careful, some people will eat anything you take them, they are the

Mikeys of the world.

It is a long process and most of us who have participated in that tasting venture are pretty thick-skinned; we don't mind being told that our new chip tastes horrible. We have to be able to say that well, that doesn't work, let's try again...

In addition to taste testing the new flavor around the plant, our marketing people will go to universities with young people, go to some of the classes, go to some of the dining halls and just see what the students think.

We also do mall intercepts, but that is later in the process. Originally, we start right here with sample bags and taste and talk about them in meetings. Then the new product evolves, but we won't go outside and do all the taste tasting until we are pretty sure internally that we have what we are after.

Our consumers are pretty savvy and our team has grown to be in tuned with what we think our consumers want.

– *Randy Bates*

Whoops! Marketing Miscues

Mistakes – see that energy bag up there. [He points to a green bag on a shelf with the letters NRG across the bag. The Golden Flake logo is nowhere to be seen on the bag.]

Red Bull was a monster hit and we thought an energy chip would be a natural. After all the energy drinks were flying off the shelves so we figured our energy chip would too. And we were thinking the NRG chips would be a good thing to do because frankly there is a fair amount of profit in it. The Red Bulls and the Monsters of the world are knocking people over with profit, energy drinks have a huge price markup and you can sell a can for three dollars compared to a can of Coke for only a dollar.

Hmm, our energy chip flopped instead and the only thing we could figure out is that the consumer is big on drinking energy products, they are not big on eating energy products –

you drink coffee, Coke.

None of the energy consuming products you have to eat, none of them have been a success. They have even tried energy jelly beans, but no energy product you have to eat has been successful – only the liquids have been successful.

– *Randy Bates*

Trends

Trends affect us, but not as much as people think. Our consumers want something that tastes good – the bottom line is we are a 'feel-good' product.

In good times and bad times, we are a feel-good product. When there is a downturn in the economy, our business actually goes up; we show an increase in sales because we are a feel-good product.

Also the consumer doesn't eat out as much they buy groceries more, they eat sandwiches more, and therefore they buy our product to go along with the sandwiches, so we show an increase in sales. When things are going good, we do okay there too, but we don't see the same increase in sales when people are out going to restaurants.

Healthy? There is a market there and when you apply it to our business it's very small and we do some, but we feel that our products are good and our products are good for you, but we firmly believe all things in moderation – our products have been around a long time and they will continue to be around a long time.

The health food trend does affect us, but not as much as people think. Our consumers want something that tastes good; the bottom line is we are a 'feel-good' product.

But we do have different versions of our products that offer healthier ways to eat. We have no-salt potato chips and we get letters every week from people with sodium restrictions and heart problems who love the product.

We have the 100-calorie packs, it's our same formula, a lot of 100-calories packs are different recipes. For instance, Oreos, but ours is the same formula, our original stuff in various size bags so the bags have 100 calories.

Most nutritionists will tell you it is not about the 100 calories, it is all about portion control. All things in moderation, so we appeal to folks and say eat our good stuff, just don't eat as much of it and that will be just as good for you, although in the back of our minds we are saying, heck it is just a five ounce bag, buy another one.

– *Randy Bates*

The importance of a brand

Brand value is total. Brand value is everything.

That is evidenced by the fact that every bag of product that we put out there has, in prominent position, the name Golden Flake. We do almost no individual category branding, like our competitors do.

For instance there are multiple brands under the Frito-Lay logo. However, everything that we have out there has Golden Flake on the bag, under the name Golden Flake, and we will do a descriptive, cheese puffs, cheese fries, cheese curls, potato chips, nachos. But our brand is so important to us, that in the past when we have tried to introduce new items that don't say Golden Flake, when we might put the logo on the back of the bag, it has not been very successful because our consumers feel good about Golden Flake.

We have done a terrific job of making sure Golden Flake is thought of and regarded highly. Our brand is our identity and our most powerful sales tool. We protect it and we work very hard at projecting a positive image day in and day out, with every employee, with all our tractors and trailers. We own our transportation system, we own over 320 trucks, but on the company's owned trucks we are very particular about presenting a very clean, neat image, trucks washed, to project the good food and our brand name.

We make an excellent quality line of salty snacks and we sell other items that we don't manufacture and sell them as a Golden Flake item to round out the merchandise. But it is important that we brand them as Golden Flake.

– *Randy Bates*

Stick With the Brand!!!

We have tried over the years to add additional names and products, look at Frito-Lay they have Lays, Fritos, Sun Chips, Doritos. They brand products with different names. But they can put the dollars behind each one of those brands. In fact the consumer might think they are different. Many people don't know that Doritos is the Frito-Lay brand or that Cheetos and Lays are all the same company.

We have played with a couple of brands, some successful, some not.

We had a Mrs. B brand chip and it was a little bit different than our normal thin crispy chips. It was a kettle chip.

But we have tried different kettle fried chips. We have tried them unsuccessfully twice. The first time we didn't want people to confuse the kettle chip with our Golden Flake chip, so we branded it differently. Called it Mrs. B.

But why did our kettle chip fail? It was a heavier thick chip. It is really what the product was like in the 30s, a heavier product. Like Cape Cod chips. I think because we have been identified with thin and crispy so long, people just go, "I like my thin and crispy Golden Flake."

In fact that is why we called it Mrs. B, because we didn't want people to open that bag and expect a thin and crispy potato chip, with the Golden Flake name.

But we also found that it takes so many dollars to put behind a new brand name that it is really hard to launch it and give it a market identity.

That is why we now put all our emphasis on Golden Flake potato chips, Golden Flake cheese curls, Golden Flake corn chips; we try to place everything under the Golden Flake banner.

If we have a corn chip, we are saying to the public, here is a subcategory of Golden Flake. We find that sticking with your main name, the name that everyone recognizes you by, works best for us and it works for most regional chip makers. If it says Golden Chip corn chips, people will just buy it, they will say, "Oh, that is Golden Flake, that is what we want."

Golden Flake has such a strong brand name down South and that is our strength.

Coach Bryant, we still have people that tell us they buy Golden Flake potato chips because Coach Bryant told them to. And that show, which we aired after every Alabama football game, has been off the air for years.

Heck, I wish we could resurrect Coach Bryant. At the university, there is a statue of Coach Bryant and on game day morning, people will put bags of Golden Flake chips at his feet at the base of that statue; over 26 years and we still have that strong association with Coach Bryant.

So we have learned that it is best to stick with our brand name and put it on everything.

We even have to be careful of making any changes in our packaging.

We changed the color on our cheese curls and we put a picture of our cow on there. Wow – we saw a dramatic decrease in our sales and you could see month by month by month the sales going down.

Finally we had to change our packaging because our salespeople would tell us that customers would ask, "Where are your cheese curls?"

And the salespeople would say, "They are right there, right

there on the shelf."

And the customers would say, "No, they're not. Where are your regular cheese curls?"

Our customers didn't make the transition to our new look. The new look that we had intended for 'our modern update'. Our little cartoon update cow. We had to go and reprint bags that had not been updated in 12 years. The bags had the same Golden Flake look we have been using year after year. And our sales immediately responded; we saw an immediate surge in our cheese curl sales.

We have a lot of people come here. They say, "Oh. We can update your package and make it so fancy."

But they don't understand that we are not going there in one step; we are making changes as we go, but we are not going from here to there in one swoop.

– *Julie McLaughlin*

Be wary of change

We do changes but we have learned that you only change one thing at a time. Frito-Lay changed to "being better for you". They changed to sunflower oil and put the sunflower burst on the package and changed the package look.

They also changed the weight and the price and their sales went straight down.

The problem is – they changed too many things. So how do you know what caused the sales to drop? They don't know what it was. Was it the price, the graphics, the oil, the weight?

We have learned the hard way, change one thing. Look at packaging design. Yeah, make it a little more modern; make some subtle change, move it over time where you want it.

But don't make it so the customer can't find it. They are looking for the red thin and crispy bag for Golden Flake. They say, "Yeah, there it is," and they don't notice that this little font changed a little. We noticed it, but you have to make changes slow and easy.

Our friends at Utz [They are also a regional chip maker.] had this little old dorky looking little girl and their packaging was very 40s and 50s; now they have changed packaging materials and I am sure they made a few subtle changes, but the package still looks awful and outdated, but guess what? They aren't going to change it – it works.

– *Mark McCutcheon*

Showcase the product

Are there ways to maximize your limited shelf space?

Yes, we call it 'win the floor, win the store'. So even though Frito-Lay pays big program fees to Krogers and Publix to get displays, you can counteract that if you build up a relationship with store managers who will allow you to put up displays for Super Bowl Sunday or other events.

That display may have to go in and out – but we will have more space, space beyond that chip section, which expands how much we can sell.

When I first started visiting stores, when I first started, the sales manager would walk through the door, head by the cash register and go right to the chip section – well that is the wrong process.

You have to think like a consumer. Where does a consumer go? Where do you go? You take your shopping cart and you go to the right, you go to the produce section. And what you look at is – who do you see first? Do you see Frito-Lay, Tom's? Lance? Or do you see us? What is your next stop in that store? Where is our next opportunity to be seen? How would you position our product so the consumer sees us as he walks through the store, not just in the chip aisle, but where else in the store should the consumer see us?

Our buys are impulse buys, we rarely, if ever – unless you are planning for a party – we're rarely on a grocery list.

So we are not on your grocery list; almost 80% of sales are impulse buys. So you have to have your stuff in the places where it will be seen, when they walk through the store.

You want them to say, "Oh, Golden Flake, I think I will get a bag."

In today's economy, how many people will skip the snack aisle? So our opportunity has to be based on our placement in the store, placement that gets us out of the snack aisle and into people's paths as they walk around the store.

End aisle merchandisers are added costs, but are very effective. It has been proven that displays on the end of aisles are much more effective than gondolas.

One reason is that our competition is not right there next to us. In the snack aisle you can shop their cheese curls or the store brand cheese curls.

But, on an end aisle display, you don't have the potential of all your competitors being right there.

— *Mark McCutcheon*

Connecting with the community

We have put 25,000 people through this plant on tours every year. Does that advertise for us? Yes.

Would our insurance carriers wish we wouldn't do it from a liability standpoint? Yes.

But we are pretty big on the education of our youth around here. Junior Achievement, we think it is pretty important for a kid to come see how something is really made, how that bag of chips ended up in their home, from fresh agricultural products that we process and that end up on the shelves. It's important for kids to see how potatoes come from the farm to here.

— *Julie McLaughlin*

Sports Marketing

We are one of the original corporate sponsors of the SEC – The Southeastern Conference, which pretty much lies on top of our market, everywhere they have a team, and we sell Golden Flake. And it was a good deal. Golden Flake and Dr. Pepper were the original sponsors when the SEC started promoting the SEC game of the week, football, basketball, baseball and so on.

We were the original sponsor of Bear Bryant and we got into sports marketing from that. The Bear Bryant show after every game was a terrific show, there has been nothing like it before or since. We had a very wide audience, but in those days, there wasn't football on every channel everyday. You wanted to see Alabama football, you watched the Bear Bryant Show. It was on every week for one hour and Golden Flake and Coke were exposed to a great audience.

That led to other sponsorships. You need your name out as much as you can. The SEC gives us great exposure. We also sponsor things like the Talladega 500, NASCAR – we sponsored for years the Tennessee Walking Horse National Tournament – a lot of loyal fans.

We try to sponsor Southern events because we do not want to sponsor somebody who goes outside the places we supply product. It makes no sense to sponsor someone who is outside our territory. The public outside our area sees our ads and goes, "Who are they?" They don't know who we are. We want to sponsor events that expose our name to the people who walk into our store and buy our product.

– *Wayne Pate*

Key Sales Tips

If you are a route salesperson looking at the store, there are five key fundamentals you must know to be successful. If every time you go into your store you can go in and say yes to all five of them, you will have a successful route.

The five key fundamentals are: position of space, service, distribution, display and good will. You must be able to go in and answer each of these fundamentals. You must be able to say, "I have position for the customer, consumer coming, I have enough space for my product so I have position and space. I provide service, in other words, I am there when I need to be there to make sure everything is stocked.

I have got my store manager happy, and he is going to come back and give me displays later on when I ask for them; he is going to take care of me when special orders come in and he is going to forgive me if I mess up every now and then.

I got the proper distribution, in other words I got the right amount of product in the right place at the right time so I can meet the needs of most of the customers coming in.

I must have the right distribution of product, make sure I don't have too much of this and not enough of that – it is a balancing act.

It takes effort – that is what route salesmanship is all about. Make sure you have position, space, service, distribution, when you leave that store.

Your section should be displayed so that you would be willing to sign your name to a piece of paper, saying, "I displayed that." If it's clean, fresh and neat, then the consumer is willing to buy off of it. You don't want your section to look picked over and not merchandised well. If you have your display looking well, then you have a better chance of selling, if the consumer likes what they see.

And then finally, a crucial point of any sales success is good will and good will is derived from performing those other four functions. If you do those first four, then good will, most of the time, will come to you from that store manager, or storeowner, and you will have a much better chance of selling your product.

Another key to good will is you gotta be yourself. You gotta go make friends and people will buy because they like you, sometimes to the point of not caring what you are bringing in there to sell just as long as they like you. In short, the service end of it, making sure your section is clean and always stocked with the right products, will get you the good will and your own personality will help sales.

We teach those all the times – those are the five pieces of success.

And those five things apply to anyone who sells.

If you can do those five things, you will have a lot of fun because it will be easy.

– *Randy Bates*

Note: The customers are the stores that Golden Flake sells to

Sales are satisfying the needs of that consumer. It is asking what the consumer wants and doing your dead level best to satisfy that expectation. Frankly, that is what we have as a mission: "Consistently satisfying the expectations of our customers, employees and stockholders by producing and selling quality snacks."

That's it, that's all we do, day in and day out. If each person in sales can go in and put themselves in the place of the person they're selling, if they know that person's needs, then the salesperson will be taken care of. If the salesperson goes in and puts their own needs ahead of the customer, they will never be successful.

I don't care how long a salesperson tries, the customer will read them like a book and that perspective customer will realize that the salesperson does not have their best interests at heart; the salesperson is just trying to make money, as opposed to going in and taking care of the needs of the customer.

You have to sell a need and that need must match the customers' needs.

– Randy Bates

Taking care of business

Most of our business is repeat customers; at least 70% of our business is repeat customers. We go in and keep the shelves full in stores and the stores, by and large, have the same consumers coming in week in and week out.

Yet, we are always looking for new business; when new stores open up, we are always the first to call on them. All the time we are pushing for new business, we don't sit on our laurels and expect our old business to take care of us; we would go out of business. You can't ride the fence; you either are going forward or backward…

We always try to push our people to be out there looking for new business. Old business is good to have, but as I was telling you before the people I am going to see tomorrow have 1700 stores that I am hoping to sell to.

We have a very good working relationship with Walmart. Walmart is space and sale; you take care of Walmart and you sell product in Walmart, you get space in Walmart.

Walmart is our largest customer, but we also make sure that it doesn't creep to be such a large animal that if we ever lost them it would cripple us. We want to make sure that we can take care of everybody that can sell a bag of chips. But Walmart is very fair, you have to explain everything you want to do and you have to justify it; but as long as you can justify and explain it, as with a lot of our large customers, we don't have any issues at all, we know where we stand with them and our other customers as well. If you can justify what you ask for, most of the times you get it.

– Randy Bates

Why grocery stores love snack foods

There is a reason grocery stores love large snack aisles. There is a lot more money to be made in snack foods than there is pork and beans. Most products in a grocery store offer the store very low margins.

But ours? They don't to have worry about it, we take care of it. They don't need box boys putting up the bags and stuff, we do it. So their margins are much greater. That is why the end aisles often feature snack food merchandising – lots of cookies and lots of snack foods. They make a lot more money off of chips than canned goods.

Plus, we guarantee the sale and if Johnny goes in there and rips open the bag, eats half of it and sticks it back, we give the store credit for that bag. If it goes out of date, we give them credit for that bag, so we guarantee the sale.

But we have less than 2% of our bags returned every year. And that is a very good percentage with a perishable item.
– *Randy Bates*

Keys to a good sales force

Dependability, trust, build up good relationships, have what is needed and enough of it available to the consumer when they need it, make sure that you have enough fresh product available that you don't miss sales. That your product is always fresh so you maximize the opportunity to satisfy the consumer.

And dependability means a lot of things. You are there when you say you are going to be there. Also do what you told them you would do. And be helpful to the customer. And be trustworthy,

You are in stores. You have to be considerate, the fact that you being there doesn't interrupt the store's operations. You are going in there where people are so you don't want to mess up what they are doing. You want to be a help to them, not a hindrance.

That's a part of being trustworthy and dependable and being somebody that the customer wants to come to their store. Being able to work the hours that need to be done to accomplish those goals. Sometimes store must be flexible.

To make yourself valuable to them. Our sales force must have one characteristic: they need to make themselves valuable to the stores.

The consumer mostly doesn't see our salespeople. They may see them in the stores, there's the Golden Flake man, but that's about it. So the people who know who we are, are the stores, our customers.

We need to be considerate of them, where we park the truck, how we get in and out of the store without being disruptive to their operation. It's the little things and they all add up.

– *Wayne Pate*

Lesson Two

We're from the government and we're here to help you

Chapter 7

Logic Flies Out of The Window

Democracy is a form of government in which it is permitted to wonder aloud what the country could do under first-class management.

– Anon

Introduction: By this portion of the book, we have discussed raw materials, storage, production, seasoning, packaging, marketing, sales, transportation, inventions, innovations and we are just touching the surface of what it takes to understand business. We still have regulations, and special interest groups and lobbying and competition and the government that we must try to get a handle on. Let's move forward and delve into all these issues that affect business.

Dealing with issues – CANCER?

To be in business, you have to be aware of the business atmosphere you are operating in. You have to be aware of issues that often come out of left field. And you have to understand the scientific literacy of the public you are dealing with, and you cannot underestimate the fear factor. For example, this case study talks about acrylamides and it all started in Sweden and has everything to do with marketing that bag of chips.

Acrylamides cause cancer, or do they? Meet your stakeholders.

Doing business is strange. It is more than numbers. It often has nothing to do with numbers. Sometimes it boils down to scanning the horizon and being aware of the issues that may impact your business and industry.

In short you have to be aware of all the stakeholders that can affect your business.

Stakeholders? Who are they?

A stakeholder is anyone that can affect your business or who is affected by your business. The obvious ones are customers, shareholders, the government, employees.

It is the ones that you are not aware of that can hurt you. For example, think about a small lab in Sweden that 'discovers' that potato chips cause cancer.

What?

About seven years ago, these Swedish scientists alarmed the snack food world by claiming that acrylamide, a compound found in foods heated at high temperatures, for instance potato chips, could cause cancer.

Enter your problem. As an executive at Golden Flake or any snack food producer, the minute anything, anywhere is suspected of causing cancer, you will find health groups, with very important sounding names, demanding that you do something about IT!!! And do it NOW!

Never mind that the studies include that magic word 'might'. Health food organizations ignore that little word and head straight for panic mode and that means potential pain for small companies like Golden Flake.

And your problem as a CEO or a 'very logical thinking business major' is that logic has very little to do with the real world of business.

A little personal experience with 'special interest groups'. Or 'studies show...'

I saw this time and time again when I was an executive speech-writer for Arizona Public Service, which built three nuclear plants. I attended rally after rally, where people raged against building any more nuclear plants, because the plants would eventually kill people. Of course, the protesters ignored the fact that all nuclear plants have containment domes which can be hit by a small plane and not even shatter.

Or that not one person, despite the media hysterics, has ever been killed in a nuclear power accident in the United States. Or the fact that if we didn't use nuclear power, that meant we had to use oil, not a very good idea, or coal, which has that nasty little habit of polluting the skies and causing black lung disease.

I mention all of this to show, again, that to be a successful business thinker, you have to be a multidimensional thinker, and realize that the best business models and economic calculations can be easily derailed by an uneducated public which has little or no scientific training, and which can easily be stampeded into panic by the media.

Am I making this up? Are Americans really scientifically illiterate and any logical argument based on science and fact will be ignored by them?

Consider this, studies show that only about 28% of American adults know enough science to understand reports in major newspapers. That means that over 70% of Americans, your customers, cannot even follow a basic science story in the newspaper.

Even more depressing is a California Academy of Sciences survey which showed that the US public is unable to pass even a basic scientific literacy test. Consider these results:

Only 53% of adults know how long it takes for the Earth to revolve around the Sun.

Only 59% of adults know that the earliest humans and dinosaurs did not live at the same time.

Only 47% of adults can roughly approximate the percent of the Earth's surface that is covered with water.

Only 21% of adults answered all three questions correctly.

The economic cost

So what?

The findings are relevant because there is an economic cost to this illiteracy. Even to a potato chip maker like Golden Flake.

Now let's return to acrylamides.

Because of shaky findings that acrylamides might cause cancer, many organizations screamed that acrylamides be banned and, if they were not banned, at least warnings had to be posted.

And in a way politicians are smarter than many MBAs. They know that their voters know little or nothing about science and they know they can look like heroes to their voters by battling the 'Big Bad Companies' like McDonald's and Frito-Lay.

(So far, Golden Fake has been able to escape the financial consequences of acrylamides, simply because they were not in California, where politicians stormed the national stage and demanded that big companies like McDonald's and Frito-Lay warn their customers that acrylamides cause cancer.)

A basic lesson – How the economy really works

Now here is a business lesson on how the economy really works.

Executives made the classic mistake of many business majors. They believed, for no apparent reason, that people were logical, and if they sat down and talked common sense to the people and the politicians, that acrylamides would 'go away'.

Whoops! Logic sometimes has nothing to do with the real world.

While business people were calmly explaining there was no problem, health groups and politicians, who know that people act on emotion, not logic, charged full speed ahead and took the 'BIG BAD' snack food companies to court.

The results?

California Attorney General Edmund G. Brown, Jr. settled lawsuits against Heinz, Frito-Lay, Kettle Foods and Lance, Inc.

after the companies agreed to slash levels of the cancer-causing chemical acrylamides in their potato chips and French fries.

Under the settlements, Frito-Lay, Inc., which sells most of the potato chips sold in California, Kettle Foods, Inc., maker of Kettle Chips, and Lance, Inc., maker of Cape Cod Chips, agreed to reduce acrylamides over a period of three years to 275 parts per billion. For Frito-Lay, this is about a 20% reduction; while for Kettle Chips, which contain far more acrylamides, this is an 87% reduction in acrylamides. Most Cape Cod chips are already near the compliance level, but one product, "Cape Cod Robust Russets", contained over 7,000 parts per billion of acrylamides, and will carry a warning label on the package or will be removed from the market.

And underestimating the public's ability to panic was costly for chip makers.

Frito-Lay will pay $1.5 million in penalties and costs; $550,000 will be forgiven if it can reduce acrylamides in its products in half the time required by the settlement. It will pay an additional $2 million if it fails to reduce acrylamides in the required time. Kettle Foods will pay $350,000 in penalties and costs, while the much smaller Lance, Inc. will pay $95,000 in fees and costs.

And recently the California Attorney General reached an agreement with Heinz, Inc., the manufacturer of Ore-Ida frozen French fries and tater tots. Heinz will pay $600,000 in penalties and costs and will change its fried potatoes to contain 50% less acrylamides.

Whoops! We were wrong

Let's repeat a key lesson here. Often economics has nothing to do with logic, everything to do with emotions. Because ironically the snack food companies were RIGHT. There is little or no danger from acrylamides.

Newer studies never uncovered links to colon cancer or breast cancer from acrylamides. A Swedish study even indicated that long-term intake of acrylamides did not raise the risk of endometrial cancer.

In short, acrylamides posed no risk to humans.

And the authors of the original study that launched the scare later admitted that the association seen between acrylamides and cancer were – whoops – a mistake. But scientists don't say "mistake". They say, "It was simply a chance finding."

A chance finding that cost potato chip makers millions of dollars.

Remember, a key component of this book is to help you see inside the world of business and how it really works.

And to remember that as a business you have many stakeholders, all who can panic at any time, sending your company into a tailspin. Even if you just make potato chips.

The Real World of Golden Flake
Golden Flake Stakeholders

[Stakeholders are anyone affected by the actions of your corporation.]

The employees are the second largest owners of the company. We have an Employee Stock Ownership Plan and through the ESOP, employees have the second largest block of stock in the company, so they are all owners of the company.

You have got your customers. Our customers are the stores – Publix and Winn-Dixie and Walmart and Krogers and Sammies or Billies and Quick Stop and this and that – those are our customers.

But beyond that, the people we have to be sure we are taking care of are our consumers. Those are the people that are buying our products. They are our stakeholders, our consumers, our customers.

We also have our suppliers. If the supplier can't make a living supplying us, they can't supply us, so we have to be smart enough to deal with people. You can always buy something cheaper, but you buy something cheaper and run everybody out of business.

But by the same token, you can take too much and run yourself out of business. So the suppliers are a critical part.

Of course the employees are shareholders and employees. And the shareholders who don't even know who we are. They own some of our stock.

And we have to be sure we are satisfying the communities we serve. Be a good corporate citizen, which is difficult in Birmingham sometimes because of all the chaos with the city and county and all of that; it is difficult. (Jefferson County is so badly run and so crooked that it recently had to declare bankruptcy and a number of county officials are in jail.)

But we have been a good corporate citizen. We pay our taxes and pay wages and payrolls. And we do that in a lot of cities. We have to be considerate to them and where we have our warehouses and where we drive our trucks. We deliver a lot of times into neighborhoods. We don't want to be perceived as bad in a neighborhood.

And stakeholders are people who drive by our plants. People don't drive by the plant very much in Birmingham; but in Ocala, I said I want this plant to look like something, and it looks nice. We have a nice long tree-lined driveway that leads up to it, beautiful landscaped lawn, beautiful building – I don't want it to look like a place, gee who would eat that product, looks like a hog pen.

I want people to drive by and say, "I bet they make good stuff in there."

And we do.

We made a decision that affected the county, one of our stakeholders. You can say, well you should keep giving the money to the county because they need the money. Well, we can't afford it, they have mismanaged it so much, and we can't afford to let them run our sewer business. We will do it ourselves.

In a sense, all the regulatory agencies are stakeholders; they have a job to do and we have to make sure that we are satisfying their requirements, and I told you how we do that by making sure that our standards are higher than theirs.

– *Wayne Pate*

Chapter 8

Unintended Consequences are Expensive

Chaos is a friend of mine.
– Bob Dylan

Introduction: So, as a businessperson, we have learned that you must know more than raw materials, production, marketing, transportation; you also must know how to deal with stakeholders and you must beware of issues, like cancer scares, that can cost your business millions of dollars. What else must you be aware of? Well, let's find out!

SOX it to me!

SOX is not only crucial economics history that you need to know to sound intelligent, but also reinforces the central theme of this book that to understand business you must realize that the real world of economics is messy and chaotic at best and you must consider all factors that will affect your company, including government regulations intended to 'help'. SOX is one such example.

The Sarbanes-Oxley Act (SOX) was pushed into law in 2002 when a bunch of corporate crooks ripped off investors. Perhaps the poster boy for these crooks was Bernie Ebbers who, through his company WorldCom, was able to milk investors out of $11 billion.

Because of the accounting scandals at WorldCom, Enron and other large public companies, Congress felt an overwhelming responsibility to protect Americans. Of course the lesson for Golden Flake and many other small companies is beware when Congress "feels an overwhelming responsibility". We will touch upon that later.

The problem that SOX tried to address wasn't just that the corporations went under; corporations do that every day. The problem was the companies had been losing money for years and, whoops, the leaders of these companies forgot to include this information on the financial statements. (By the way, to even come across as halfway financially literate, you must be able to read financial statements. If you can't even read a basic balance sheet, check out the chapter that walks you through Golden Flake's financial statements.)

Like many good ideas coming out of Congress, SOX was supposed to end all corporate corruption, but then again World War I was the war to end all wars.

Obviously SOX did not end corruption. Bernie Madoff, who holds the dubious distinction of being the greatest conman of all time, was able, after SOX was passed, to bilk investors out of $50 billion dollars, in the belief that if you are going to screw your investors, do it right.

Golden Flake, like most small companies, had a major issue with SOX, because, instead of introducing new products or paying more dividends or increasing salaries, it had to use money to pay accountants.

Remember, and this is a crucial theme running throughout this book, Golden Flake must sell a bag of chips for $2. And every time it has to pay accountants, Golden Flake must cut expenses somewhere else, be it in marketing, sales, production, salaries. And accountants, much like lawyers, do not improve productivity or help to introduce new products.

Ironically, the SEC predicted that the costs of complying with the SOX regulations would only cost companies about $91,000 a year.

Whoops. Studies showed that after SOX went into law, public companies were spending $4.4 million on average to comply with SOX.

The Real World of Golden Flake

Sarbanes-Oxley was an act drafted with good intentions by the government. But they didn't really think what impact it would have on small companies. At Golden Flake, we are a small non-accelerated publicly traded company; we don't have to have external auditors to say our books are fair. They made some revisions to the act and this past year we went through our first year of management assessment. It was more streamlined.

Before they started streamlining the process, we had to do it like an IBM. Our small company had to jump through the same hoops as a large corporation. That costs us a lot of money, looking at everything, making sure a signature was three times in one little box, not outside the box. The government was micromanaging us. And remember we are a smaller company.

Every month we have a meeting, we talk about financial statements every month but – because of the Sarbanes-Oxley act – Randy, Dave, Jim Moore and I would have to meet for a disclosure meeting beyond that. Just to make it legal. We had to talk about what we just talked about two days before. We had to test everything using all the controls the government now required and that we had already passed the first time.

We were hitting everything with a sledgehammer rather than hitting the nails with a small hammer and the spikes with a sledgehammer.

I don't really blame the government for this. I blame Bernie Ebbers, Kenneth Lay, Richard Scrushy for thinking they were above the law.

We have a very clean balance sheet. It's complex, but it is very simple from a financial standpoint. But we had to again jump through hoops that Sarbanes-Oxley had placed on us and that of course caused us a lot of additional costs that did not add to the bottom line.

And we had to deal with additional costs, implementation of new accounting and record-keeping software, increased business expenses related to information technology, accounting, and law.

Those additional regulatory costs did not add to help our shareholders; it took earnings per share away from them. I estimate that just complying with Sarbanes-Oxley, when it first came out, cost us about a million a year.

We could have taken that million tied into the SOX compliance costs and sent that million out as dividends, charity donations, or reinvestments to further grow Golden Flake.

— *Patty Townsend*

Chapter 9

Flexibilty Saves the Day

The entrepreneur always searches for change, responds to it, and exploits it as an opportunity.
– Peter F. Drucker

Introduction: By this phase of the book, you should understand that a businessperson, besides just producing and selling a product, must deal with a number of outside forces. We have given the examples of cancer scares and government regulations. Now, let's look at another example of what business leaders must deal with.

Down the Drain: Why Golden Flake must be in the water business

There is a great economics term. *Ceteris Paribus*. And if you violate *ceteris paribus* you draw the wrong conclusion.

In Latin *ceteris paribus* means 'other things constant'. Economists use *ceteris paribus* when describing what will happen if you make one change and all other variables associated with your decision stayed the same.

For example, a *ceteris paribus* statement would be the following: "*Ceteris paribus*, a decrease in the price of cars will cause buyers to buy more cars."

This is obviously not true because so many other factors enter into buying cars.

In short, we live in a dynamic world where the other variables do change. Therefore do not assume *ceteris paribus* in economic decision-making.

And that is one mistake the Jefferson County Board made. Onward.

How to increase sewer rates by 300%

Good intentions do not equal success. Golden Flake and every other business in Jefferson County, Alabama learned that the expensive way.

In fact, Golden Flake, which used to spend $20,000 every month on water and sewer fees, saw this increase to over $100,000 a month. Remember, as we constantly stress throughout this book, you can only raise your prices if you are the big boy on the block. If Frito-Lay, which dominates the chip market, keeps the price of potato chips at $1.99 a bag, Golden Flake cannot raise their price. This means that to pay the outrageous increase in their monthly sewer and water bill, Golden Flake must either reduce costs, which could include layoffs, or find creative ways to deal with the problem.

But first, let's take a look at a real world case which will teach you about do-gooders and bankers and bonds and all that cool stuff.

Do-gooders often do more harm than good. That is what happened to Jefferson County and what started the downward spiral towards the county being forced into bankruptcy and Golden Flake facing unimaginable water bills.

In December 1993, three citizens sued the Jefferson County Commission, saying untreated sewage was being dumped into the Black Warrior and Cahaba rivers during heavy rains. Whoops! This violated the federal Clean Water Act. And these citizens had a point – no one likes to swim in brown water flavored with urine.

The US Environmental Protection Agency jumped in, well not the river, but the lawsuit. The county agreed to build a sewer system to collect overflows and clean the water.

So far, so good. We are going to have a clean river, but wait. Like all economic decisions, there is that one little nagging question. Who is going to pay for this neat new sewer system?

Well, Golden Flake and everyone, including single mothers,

would pay for it. Single mothers would see their monthly water and sewer bills increase to over $200 a month. Golden Flake would pay even more, think millions here, as they were the second top customer of the sewer system.

The way it works is pretty simple – to improve the sewer system, Jefferson County sells bonds to investors. Let say the new sewer system will cost $100. Well, I sell a bond to an investor and he gives me $100. Of course, at the end of three years, the investor wants me to pay him back the $100 and interest. So at the end of three years we will pay the investor $125.

Where does the county get the money to pay the investor back?

Easy – just raise the average sewer bill by $5 and use that money to pay the investor back.

Sounds simple and most economic ideas are until people get a 'better idea'.

Whoops, the bankers and Jefferson Country had 'a better idea'.

The county sold $2.9 billion in bonds to raise money for the project. That's a lot of money, but our $100 example still explains the basic concept. If you bought a Jefferson County Sewer Bond you would get your original money back plus an additional 5.25% in interest.

In 2002, with municipal bond interest rates near a 34-year low, bankers told Jefferson County officials they could save millions of dollars by refinancing their sewer debt.

Remember the housing debacle – how everyone bought a house because adjustable rate mortgages were low and you could get into a house for $500 a month. No one thought that the adjustable rates would triple and your house payment would triple to $1,500 a month, forcing you into foreclosure or bankruptcy.

You guessed it – Jefferson County converted their bonds to adjustable rates and threw out the fixed 5% rate. Jefferson County issued $3 billion of adjustable-rate bonds.

As many people have learned, banks talk you into refinancing your mortgage, changing from an adjustable rate to a fixed rate, not because they love you, but because they get a percentage off the top. Remember you never ask the barber if you need a haircut and you never ask the bank if you need a loan.

In fact, these new Jefferson County bonds earned the banks about $55 million in fees. When the whole mess was done, Jefferson County ended up paying over $120 million in fees to bankers.

It gets even more complicated with bankers taking more fees and Jefferson County issuing more bonds and politicians taking bribes and the cost of the sewer system doubling and soon the debt had reached into the billions and the only way that Jefferson County could pay it off was to double and triple and quadruple water and sewer bills.

And Golden Flake couldn't pay those bills and sell potato chips for $2 a bag and stay in business. So Golden Flake got off Jefferson County sewer system, dug its own well and installed its own treatment facility.

In other words, to make potato chips, Golden Flake had to go into the water business. And once again, you can see why running any business is about so much more than just selling a product.

The Real World of Golden Flake
High water usage

Making potato chips is a high water user, the slicer is a high water user and we are looking at a slicing system that will cut back on the water use. The slicing area is a high water user because in the slicing area you have to wash most of the starch off of the potatoes before you put them in the fryer and you have to get a good flow of water going.

But we do get the starch out of the water and we recirculate about 40% of the water.

Five years from now, through technology, we will be able to recycle about 90% of the water and we will be looking at washers that will use a lot less water.

The corn wash, once you precook the corn, then you have to run it through a washer mill that brushes the husk off the corn, off the outside of the corn so it will mill and grind, so you have high water usage in that the corn washer.

– David Jones

Coping with government costs or How to think ahead

You look for the most efficient ways to do anything you can, so you don't have as many dollars going out. But we don't have an unlimited budget and resources are limited. Yes, new packaging machines allow us to be more efficient, but then we have to cut poor Julia's budget in marketing.

We try to plan ahead the best we can. You can't always predict what the county is going to do; it is like a wild animal running around in a room.

One thing we do know, back from five years ago when they screwed the sewers up, that we knew every year that they would raise the rate by some amount.

We looked at our water usage; our sewer bill is based on the water we use. They read the water meter, then they calculate from the gallons you use how many of those gallons went down the drain as far as water. So we started looking five years ago to slowly find ways and equipment that we could purchase to limit the amount of water that we were using so we could actually make a profit.

So you have a whole new dynamic when you are looking at equipment, it's got to be efficient and save water and electricity. The less water we use the better; it is an ongoing process. When you look at capital expenditures, and I am only allowed to spend so much money, Patty won't let me spend everything I want to spend.

We analyze everything we might buy. For example potato peelers, it's one of those things, if you peel a lot of potatoes you use a lot of water, so the main thing you have to figure out, are there potato peelers out there that use less water and the answer to that is YES.

So we try to put new peelers in the capital expenditure budget that use less water and we try to do that with everything that uses a lot of water. For example, water spray nozzles. So we make sure that we have the water spray nozzle people come in and check once a year on our nozzles. We ask is there a better way or a better nozzle that uses less water to get the job done.

There are all sorts of things we do like that; we recycle a lot of water in the plant so we don't use a continuous stream of fresh water. We reuse water; we take starch out of it.

We reclaim the starch and sell it. But the fact is, the less water we use the better. We are not the only ones looking at it; industry wide, the snack food industry is looking at conserving. I guess you could say it is part of the growing green movement.

We know there is equipment out there now that will cut our utility costs down; in the last five years that is all we have been doing, trying to figure out ways to use less water.

In regards to the sewer system, we know that we can't pass on a 367% increase to our customers, to the guy that goes out and buys a 99 cent bag of chips; he is not going to take a 367% hit.

Fortunately, we have friends in the industry that we talk with and ask what you are doing in this area. We try to look out ahead and control what we can control. There are certain things we can't control; we can't control what they are going to charge on sewer costs, but we can control what we put down the sewer.

– *Mark McCutcheon*

Golden Flake, government and water – supply your own water

We use about 300 gallons of water a minute. (The average person uses about 70 gallons a day.) We used to buy millions of gallons of water a year from the county. We did primary treatment on it, and then sent it back to the county. But with both water and sewer climbing at more than 100% a year in some cases, we decided to build our own well. Heck, we will supply our own water.

Our Birmingham plant sits in Jones Valley and there is a great aquifer table in Jones Valley and we were able to tap into that aquifer and we have a well, with pure clean water that really doesn't even require chlorination, but we do.

Then we received a permit from the Environmental Protection Agency to treat our wastewater and discharge it into the stream. We will not have to go to the county to treat it. Now the county is going to lose a lot of revenue, but it is going to save us over a million dollars a year. That's just in wastewater alone.

The well cost us several thousand dollars but when you consider how much you are saving, it pays back pretty quick. When the county is going to charge you four to five million dollars a year, it pays back pretty quickly.

– Wayne Pate

Escaping the Jefferson County sewer

We continued in Birmingham to do primary treatment on our sewer water and let the county do the other treatments, until the whole sewer system spun out of control.

Then we said – looks like we have to do our own sewer treatment too.

The Japanese developed, because of their concentration of large groups of people in small areas, those high-rise apartment buildings. They had to have some method of treating sewerage and getting clean water and they developed a system which we are using down there and it can give pure clean water and recycle for thousands of people that live in the same place.

And that technology, we bought when we were building a treatment plant and we were putting better water into the stream than they ever had in the stream, other than the rainwater. And we went to the environmental people who typically resist any discharge into the streams and told them we were going to do it, showed them what we could do, and they applauded us.

So if we have to buy water, we won't have to pay for sewerage. It wasn't free. We had to make a big investment and we will have to pay to operate it, but even paying for all that we are going to end up with a payback of four years or less.

And we have a sewer treatment plant right on the facility; we will still give the county the sanitary sewer, the restrooms and all. We separated the streams.

In short, we still plan to buy some water from the county, for our employees' personal use and that type of thing; we don't have to do that either, but we will. Trying to be a good citizen I guess.

But we couldn't afford their sewer debacle and had to take steps so we weren't paying for their mistakes.

– *Wayne Pate*

Start of water issues

I went to work at Golden Flake in 1968. I had been at Texaco and I didn't know what I was going to do when I came; they said they had about 13 things they needed me to do.

After about three months they asked me to head up the development of a corn chip area. Along the way there we got a notice from the county that said they were going to have to start charging us a surcharge for BOD and solids in our wastewater. BOD measures the amount of oxygen in your waste-water.

The county was going to start charging us for those things that they had to get out of the water; oxygen in the water was going to kill the fish.

And when I went to Golden Flake, we were paying $800 a month for water and sewer. Keep that number in mind when I tell you what happened. So the county sent us some letters and they were going to have to start charging surcharges, they were going to start charging us for what they were taking out of our wastewater. I found out that our surcharge, alone, was going to be over $17,000 a month.

I was shocked; when you go from $800 a month to over $17,000 a month, just for a surcharge, that is shocking.

I immediately began to working on that: how can we treat our own water, how can we reduce that? There was nothing available.

So we started to work with a company to develop a treatment system to take out the solids, to weed them out. We didn't worry about the BOD. By removing the solids, we got a lot out.

Keep in mind that the county was under the gun with the EPA and they came to us as an industry. I found that out and I also found out that they had gone to other industries in town, like the Pepsi and Coke bottlers. And it was a shock to all of us, to have these huge surcharge fees; none of us were prepared for this.

So we went down to the county and talked to the county commissioners. We had three good county commissioners and we said, "Really we want to comply, but we need some help, we need some time because we don't have any means to do what you want to do, we can't afford to pay what you want."

So they gave us some time. During that time we got a system to help us reduce the solids and the waste going down the sewer.

But through the years they have been growing and kept growing – sewer and water fees have gotten to the point where they are ridiculous.

– *Wayne Pate*

Government regulations can hamper the best-laid plants

And we use so much water and sewer, before we build a plant anywhere, we check out the water and sewer infrastructure.

We built a plant in Ocala in 1984; the county told us they could handle all our water, all our sewer, all our water treatments. They could do all of that.

Well, we went ahead and drilled two wells at the Ocala plant; we are regulated by everyone down there, St. Johns River Authority and the Florida Department of Environmental Regulation and everyone has to have a hand in it. Florida is very particular about their resources.

But when we went down to get the letter from the city about handling our sewerage, the city manager said, "Wayne. I can't do it."

I said, "Wait a minute, we bought the land and made the investment down here based on you being able to do that."

He said, "I'm sorry, but the Department of Regulations has me tied up. They won't even let me discharge water."

Well, Ocala had the capacity to handle our sewer; government regulations just wouldn't let them do it.

So we had to learn quickly about the sewer business. So we bought a biological treatment plant for Ocala and we started, the very first day, to do not only primary, but secondary treatment of our sewerage. So we learned a lot about sewerage down there.

– *Wayne Pate*

Chapter 10

Ethanol Realities

Political pandering comes in all shapes and sizes, but every four years the presidential primary bring us in contact with its purest form – praising ethanol subsidies amid the corn fields of Iowa.
– John Sununu

Introduction: Look, we're just making chips here. That is what the people at Golden Flake want to do, because they do it well. But as we have seen, it is a strange world out there, a much different one, than the one in Econ 101, where they teach about supply and demand, but they don't teach about cancer scares, government regulations and even having to build your own sewer system. Can the world of business get any stranger? Oh yes! Read on.

Ethanol, Lobbying and You Gotta Wonder

Ethanol is one of those fascinating subjects which show how the real world affects that bag of chips you buy.

First, what is ethanol?

It's alcohol. You know the kind that you make in stills. You take some corn and ferment it, run it through a still and you have grain alcohol.

But you can't drink ethanol because it is denatured. That means they put nasty chemicals in it so you can't drink it.

I know, sounds like a waste of good alcohol to me too.

But environmentalists say ethanol is good because you can mix it with gasoline and use it in your car. It is supposed to make gasoline burn cleaner and if we make our own ethanol, made it from American-grown corn, we can reduce our dependency on foreign oil.

Hmm?

We will touch upon that later. Is ethanol really the energy savior for Americans?

Let's put it this way.

Corn farmers want you to believe so.

Okay – let's touch upon another basic economics rule we have touched on before. You never ask the barber if you need a haircut. What do you think he will say?

So corn farmers tell Congress that ethanol is good and will help stop the greenhouse effect and make cars run smoother and we will all be in energy heaven if we listen to them.

So Congress listens to the farmers and passes a bill which says that 25% of the corn crop must be used for ethanol.

Which means that 25% of the corn crop cannot be used to make corn chips. Which means that Golden Flake must pay more for corn. Which means it affects the price of the corn chips you buy.

Or as Bill Gates of Microsoft fame explained it, "If you are using first-class land for bio-fuels, then you're competing with the growing of food. And so you are actually spiking food prices by moving energy production into agriculture."

Chapter 11

What is Lobbying and Why Do I Need to Know About It?

Few relationships are as critical to the business enterprise itself as the relationship to government. The manager has responsibility for this relationship as part of his responsibility to the enterprise itself. To a large extent the relationship to government results from what businesses do or fail to do.
– Peter Drucker

Introduction: If you take a basic economics class, that silly professor stands up there and tells you about the free market system and how the price you pay for a bag of Golden Flake potato chips is determined by the law of supply and demand.

Actually, we have just seen that the prices of many things are not determined by market forces, but by government mandates.

If the government mandates that 25% of the corn crop be used for ethanol, that limits the supply of corn. The government mandate, not market forces, has driven up your bag of chips.

But let's see how government mandates come about through lobbying.

Our first question: Is Making Ethanol Effective?
The quick answer is no. Here is why.

- David Pimentel, a professor of ecology at Cornell University who has been studying grain alcohol for 20 years, and Tad Patzek, an engineering professor at the University of California, Berkeley, co-wrote a recent report which estimates that making ethanol from corn requires 29% more fossil energy than the ethanol fuel itself actually contains. The two scientists calculated all the fuel inputs for ethanol production – from the diesel fuel for the tractor planting the corn, to the fertilizer put in the field, to the energy needed at the processing plant – and found that ethanol is a net energy-loser.

- Eight billion gallons of ethanol will do little to reduce oil imports. Eight billion gallons is nothing when you realize that America burns more than 134 billion gallons of gasoline each year. Eight billion gallons might reduce America's overall oil consumption by 0.5%.

- The General Accounting Office has concluded that "ethanol's potential for substituting for petroleum is so small that it is unlikely to significantly affect overall energy security." That's still true today.

- Over the next five years, $5.7 billion in federal tax credits will support the ethanol market – a boon to Midwest corn growers.

- 14% of the corn crop was used to produce ethanol in 2006. This will reach 30% by 2013. This reduces the production of other foods like potatoes.

- Food inflation will rise by 7 to 8% over the next few years, as up to 40% of our corn and 30% of our vegetable oils are diverted from our food supplies.

- Corn prices were once driven by market forces. Today they are artificially driven up by a government mandate. In 2004, before the mandates were imposed, the cost of corn hovered around $2 per bushel. Now it is close to $8 per bushel.

- With ethanol production using 24% of the total corn crop, roughly 20 million acres of cropland in the United States alone is being devoted to a non-food product.

- Corn ethanol has about the same effect on US motor gasoline consumption as proper inflation of passenger car tires.

- An average ethanol refinery emits dozens of dangerous chemicals into the air, such as toluene, ethylbenzene, acetone, formaldehyde, acetaldehyde, acrolein, benzene, styrene, and furfural. In line with the current schizophrenic attitude towards ethanol production, the US Environmental Protection Agency proposes allowing ethanol refineries to increase their legal air emissions, from 100 to 250 tons per year.

Is ethanol a bad idea? It appears to be. In fact, Golden Flake knew this years ago when it tried making ethanol to sell. See the interview at the end of this chapter for information about Golden Flake's foray into the world of ethanol.

If Ethanol is such a bad idea, why-oh-why????

As always, welcome back to Potato Chip Economics and all the things that affect the price of that bag of chips you buy.

Many experts agree that ethanol is not one of the government's best ideas and it is going to cost taxpayers billions to subsidize this bad idea and will increase the cost of corn that Golden Flake must pay for corn chips.

Yet, Congress imposed a Renewable Fuel Standard (RFS) mandate that has forced the gasoline industry to mix massive amounts of corn-based ethanol into the nation's fuel supply. In 2007, Congress nearly doubled that mandate to require nine billion gallons of ethanol be blended into gas in the near future.

Then why was it passed?

Welcome to the world of lobbying. Where members of the corn lobby stand outside the congressman's door and wring their hands and say – "Oh the poor farmer, he is the backbone of America and we must help him" or "Global warming will kill us all and thank GOD we have ethanol to put in our gas to slow down that horrible fate!"

Well actually there are not just regular people standing

outside the congressman's door. They are lobbyists and are highly paid by people like the corn lobby to pitch ideas to Congress.

Oh that is crazy. Why should any congressman listen to the corn lobby? It is called campaign contributions. Consider these facts:

- 20 members of the Senate Agriculture, Nutrition and Forestry Committee collected more than $8 million in campaign contributions from the farm sector while their 46 House counterparts have received over $4 million.
- The House Agriculture Committee's former top-ranking Democrat, Charles Stenholm of Texas, lobbies on behalf of agriculture interests too. In all, at least 19 congressional aides who worked on the 2002 farm bill have taken jobs as agriculture lobbyists or with commodity groups or farm organizations.
- Rep. Henry Bonilla, R-Texas, chairman of the House appropriations subcommittee, received $300,000 from the farm sector, and Sen. Saxby Chambliss, R-GA, chairman of the Senate Agriculture Committee, received $287,000.
- And there are practical considerations. Farmers vote. And in states dependent on agriculture those votes can swing a race.

Hey, let's be honest. If I were running for Congress and someone offered me that kind of money, heck, I would listen to them while whistling Dixie standing on my head if they wanted me to.

The point is that many rules and regulations, like the ethanol mandates, have nothing to do with the free market system; but rather have everything to do with throwing money at the right congressman. And these mandates directly affect our world of potato chip economics, by making corn more expensive to buy, thus raising the price of corn. Plus the ethanol mandate limited the supply of potatoes because farmers rushed off to raise corn. Which raises the price of potatoes.

Does lobbying work?

Well you figure it out

In the real world, the National Corn Growers Association pays a lobbying firm over half a million a year just to push for laws that will make corn farmers rich. And the government gives corn farmers more than $10 billion in subsidies each year. Now that is a great return on your investment!

How big is lobbying and how does it affect Golden Flake in other areas?

Quote: Lobbying is like the fourth branch of government. It's a very powerful part of our government and our democracy.
– *Roberta Baskin*

Let's start off with the size of lobbying. It is big. Really, really big.

In addition to campaign contributions to elected officials and candidates, companies and organizations spend billions of dollars each year to lobby Congress and federal agencies. There are over 30,000 lobbyists in Washington, DC alone.

$3.27 billion a year is spent by American business on lobbyists to persuade Congress to support their causes. According to Open Secrets, an organization that tracks lobbying firms, there is big money in lobbying.

For example – the table below lists some of the top lobbying firms in Washington, DC and their income over a decade.

Lobbying Firm	Total
Patton Boggs LLP	$320,642,000
Cassidy & Assoc	$287,945,000
Akin, Gump et al	$263,265,000
Van Scoyoc Assoc	$210,248,000
Williams & Jensen	$154,784,000

Hogan & Hartson	$141,224,162
Ernst & Young	$136,087,237
Quinn Gillespie & Assoc	$123,993,500
PMA Group	$115,780,578
Barbour, Griffith & Rogers	$114,550,000
Greenberg Traurig LLP	$111,328,249
Holland & Knight	$102,709,544
PriceWaterhouseCoopers	$94,714,084
Alcalde & Fay	$89,050,660
Verner, Liipfert et al	$88,595,000
Dutko Worldwide	$88,276,766
Carmen Group	$87,350,000
PodestaMattoon	$81,165,000
Clark & Weinstock	$81,125,000
Timmons & Co	$76,983,833

Let's look at some big spenders

Oh boy! Let's start off with another chart! This chart represents what some of the big boys spend in just one year to influence Congress.

US Chamber of Commerce	$15,476,000
Exxon Mobil	$9,320,000
Pharmaceutical Rsrch & Mfrs of America	$6,910,000
Chevron Corp	$6,800,000
Lockheed Martin	$6,482,462
Pfizer, Inc.	$6,140,000
ConocoPhillips	$5,980,935
National Association of Realtors	$5,757,000
AT&T Inc.	$5,134,873
Verizon Communications	$4,940,000
General Electric	$4,766,000
American Medical Association	$4,355,000
Blue Cross/Blue Shield	$4,317,818

American Hospital Association	$4,287,176
AARP	$4,080,000
Southern Co	$3,680,000
BP	$3,610,000
Altria Group	$3,580,000
Eli Lilly & Co	$3,440,000
Marathon Oil	$3,380,000

And this affects Golden Flake?

So there is a quick chart of some of the biggest spenders on Capital Hill. Note that whatever agendas they push will affect Golden Flake and the price of potato chips. Note the number of oil companies lobbying Congress – Marathon, Conoco, Chevron, Exxon. If Congress passes stricter pollution laws and restricts drilling, this raises the price of gasoline. And remember that Golden Flake drives trucks all over the Southeast. And that every potato chip bag is made from oil.

Also note the number of health care companies spending tons of money to influence Congress. They include Eli Lilly & Company, Pharmaceutical Researchers and Manufacturers, Pfizer, American Medical Association, Blue Cross/Blue Shield and the American Hospital Association. They are up in Washington fighting against health care reform. And if they get their way, Golden Flake may see the health insurance premiums it pays for employees keep increasing and again that affects Golden Flake's bottom line.

Also note the number of electric companies including Southern Company lobbying Congress. Southern Company provides electricity to Golden Flake and Southern Company, with other electric companies, is trying to stop Congress from passing more pollution laws. If Congress passes more laws stating that utilities must have stricter emission controls on their plants to stop global warming, Southern Company and the other utilities must spend millions to retrofit their plants with pollution devices.

This cost of course will be passed onto Southern Company's customers. Oh wait, that would be Golden Flake.

This is not to say that lobbying is a bad thing. If the gas companies can convince Congress not to limit oil exploration, if the power companies can convince Congress not to put additional pollution controls on their plants, this will, in the end, save Golden Flake money.

You never saw this connection coming!

As we study Potato Chip Economics, the great thing is all the twists and turns that we take. All the factors that influence what you pay for that bag of chips and what it takes just to get that bag of chips to the market.

Remember the National Corn Growers Association? The one that lobbied for the ethanol bills?

Well, they argued that ethanol would reduce the amount of gasoline that we use. Plus ethanol is great for the environment.

But the National Corn Growers Association is asking every corn grower to lobby Congress to increase domestic production of fossil fuels by opening the Arctic National Wildlife Reserve and the Outer Continental Shelf for exploration and production, and by drilling everywhere on US territory for oil and gas.

Why?

Because farmers depend on natural gas, coal, and petroleum. They use nitrogen derivatives and other fertilizers to produce corn. Lots of corn.

Corn farming devours fertilizers. Nitrogen fertilizers account for roughly half the total energy input per acre of harvested corn and are made from natural gas.

Enter Golden Flake again. They want the cost of fertilizer to stay stable. A rise in any production cost means another price increase in raw materials that Golden Flake may or may not be able to pass onto you.

The Real World of Golden Flake
Ethanol and the Cost of Corn

The federal government, in its infinite wisdom, has dictated that in the near future eventually a full 33% of the corn that is produced is flipped to ethanol. That is geometrically higher than anything else they have ever done and so that puts pressure on using corn for food. There will not be that much corn for food if it is going to ethanol.

Corn prices, because of this new government mandate, are going to moderate dramatically and, yes, they might moderate down some in the given economy, but as long as the Feds are saying you are going to put that much corn into ethanol, corn farmers are going to grow corn for ethanol. Why not? If you grow corn for ethanol, the Feds are giving you a guaranteed profit through subsidies and tax cuts.

– *David Jones*

There was a time in our history here, back in the early 80s, late 70s, when we went through this energy crisis before, when OPEC cut us off, we made moonshine here at Golden Flake. Ethanol is really just moonshine, with a nasty chemical thrown in, so you can't drink it.

The Feds gave us the license – we made gasohol here – but the point is we could not make it profitably and we had a source of energy, the steam coming from our plant. We had a source of raw material and we could not make ethanol profitable. The only way it can be made profitable is for the federal government to come in and subsidize it – it is the same way it is today.

Think about that, in the 80s we had a federal and state permit to make gasohol and we had a stainless steel still, we made 160 proof. We had waste corn, waste potatoes and waste heat, we made some pretty mean moonshine, and we could not make a profit, without subsidies.

I know technology has improved but I am sorry, a still is still a still. Senator Sessions came here and that is the big thing we talked about, the ethanol and we are saying, that is silly, we need food before fuel.

The ethanol mandate, politically it sounds wonderful, practically it sounds horrible.

All ethanol has done is drive the cost of food up. And if you are a wheat farmer, potato farmer, and you see the government paying you to grow corn, heck you going to think about growing corn and that impacts the price of potatoes and wheat – the law of supply and demand creeps in.

– *Mark McCutcheon*

How government mandates undermine the free market system – a basic lesson in how the real world of economics really works

In business we have to be flexible and adjust to the changing economy. The government doesn't do that. Once it makes an edict, it can't be flexible and change it on the spot. It might take years to change it; meanwhile companies like ours are affected in a negative way and we send Washington taxes that we could use to hire more people and make more product.

Let's look at ethanol. I know we have chatted about it, but it illustrates the long-term effect of shortsighted mandates.

The ethanol mandate is ongoing; we are working to get it lowered, we are doing that through our snack food association and by talking directly to our Congressmen.

But, as I said a mandate is not flexible. And what may have been good for the economy a few months ago may be bad for it now. Look at how drastically our economy has shifted but the ethanol mandates are unable to adjust to the current economy.

Well, when the government started subsiding ethanol plants and demanded that the use of corn be turned into ethanol that really started the price of corn up and up and up.

Now at first the mandates were insignificant because we had a huge carry-over of corn from year to year. We grew more corn than what could be consumed in this country.

However, beginning about three years ago, we started exporting more corn around the world. And as conditions changed and the population of countries grew they couldn't produce enough corn for themselves. China being one of those countries that we export a lot of corn to.

So you had more corn exports going out. Sure you had a rising corn crop but you also had a lot of that corn crop going into ethanol, so between the exports and ethanol, all of sudden we don't have any carry-over from growing year to growing year anymore.

In fact we were really afraid at the beginning of June that we would run out of corn before August in this country. August is when you really start your crop harvesting, and that is how small the carry-over was.

All during this time when the surplus of corn was going down and down and down, the demand was going up in this country due to the ethanol mandates. You had a rising corn price, all the farmers are going ecstatic over this; they are growing all the corn they can get their hands on.

Basically the last few years it has been some of the biggest harvests of corn since World War II.

The problem is with the exports and the ethanol; we are going to be faced pretty much with same situation again: a corn shortage and we won't have enough corn to make it to August.

The good part is, if you want to call it a good part, with the financial meltdown, a lot of the corn prices were being held up by hedge funds. Investors were hedging their bets that the price of corn was going to continue to go up and they would buy a futures contract saying, "Hey, it is going up and it is going to keep going up and up and up..."

Well, when the meltdown occurred, the hedge funds started having to liquidate their positions due to the fact that they were getting cash calls from their investors, and as a result the prices of all the commodities have fallen dramatically – and I guess you could say they're to the area where the prices could be supported where they are right now.

The prices are not down as low as they were three or four years ago, but they are down to a more realistic level. As a result, Golden Flake will have the opportunity to buy at a little better price now than we could have done a few years ago.

But getting back to the point how the free market system is really driven by so many factors, government mandates, investors trying to get rich, the growth of China's population – and these all affect us as a buyer of corn for our corn chips.

And getting back to government mandates, if you can't make it in the real world, you go bankrupt.

But the government cannot let ethanol producers go bankrupt. That would be a black eye on the government and their ethanol mandate.

There was a story in the Wall Street Journal the other day, where one of the largest ethanol producers is on the verge of bankruptcy and the federal government is going to do what? It is going to give them a bailout.

The reason that they are in trouble, they went ahead and contracted corn at a real high price and now the price of corn is way down and as a result they are stuck having to accept these loads of high priced corn and won't be able to make any money off of it.

– *David Jones*

Ethanol: You can't make a profit!!!

We have been, we are not now, but we have been a licensed

distiller of ethanol. The Alabama Liquor and Alcohol Board, we got a license. Interestingly our current President's father was the agent we dealt with. But we decided several years ago, when the first excitement came about ethanol, that we could make ethanol. Twenty, 25 years ago, ethanol was the next great thing.

We said okay and I started going to seminars about ethanol and we had the raw materials, we had potato starch, potato skins, potato peelings, corn waste – all this raw material that will make ethanol. We had waste heat, waste energy going up the stack, the steam left over from cooking. So we had what it takes to ferment and distill and we had the raw materials to make ethanol.

And as I went to the seminars and people started talking about all they were going to do to make ethanol, I said there isn't any way. I don't believe it. They aren't going to be able to do that and make it work out.

We built a still. I have some ethanol here. Pure white clean – white lightening.

We got our research done. Now we know we can do it, we know what is required. Now what is it going to cost us? I got one of the top engineering firms in Birmingham to give me an estimate, a cost on building such a plant. They had built several plants, that's why I called them.

So I called the engineering firm and they took their time and effort to give us an estimate on what it would cost to build an ethanol plant and use all the raw material we had, the waste, and they gave me a price of two million dollars. I remember the number, two million dollars for the fermentation and distilling of the raw materials we had.

"Well," I said, "I wonder if he's right?"

I have traveled a lot and I have friends all over the world and I had a friend in Germany. I said I am going to find out. I know that the Germans in World War II made ethanol from potatoes. I know they did. I am going to find out. They may still be doing that.

I called my friend and he said in his German accent, "I don't know, but I have a friend. Let me call him."

Two hours later Heinz calls me back and says, "Wayne, I have a friend who built a plant almost the same size you are talking about and in US dollars it will cost two million dollars to build."

I knew then that those people who were getting into ethanol and were going to have to buy biomass and energy would never make it work, because we had free energy and free raw material and we couldn't make it work.

So unless the price stays very high, it is going to be very difficult to make ethanol work. If you are like Archer Daniels Midland and you are making ethanol as a byproduct of the corn milling process, which is where you make your money and ethanol is a waste product, you can make some revenue from. ADM is the largest producer of alcohol in the country; they might make it work.

But to start off from scratch to make ethanol from corn grains? I think it is going to be difficult.

– *Wayne Pate*

Beyond ethanol: Other governmental impacts

When you look at a bag of chips, how much is that government added cost? That is more than people realize. How do you define government costs? Just look at the basics.

It took fuel to get the chips to the store, so we have gas taxes, road taxes. And we have city business licenses. We have a tremendous number of food permit licenses; every small town we do business in, we have a food license. It may be only 15 dollars, but that is still time and effort. We have to go to apply and pay for this food permit in every small town.

Business taxes doubled this year in Birmingham; they just

doubled. And that affects our competitive standpoint. We can't raise the price of our chips.

Remember Frito-Lay is the big dog in the territory and they set the prices. They have no competition west of the Mississippi so they can sell it for what they want to in Colorado and use that profit to go against us and sell chips for 'buy one, get one' free in the South or the Northeast.

They can do that quite effectively and hold prices down to hurt us, so local things like taxes do have an impact here and with the county almost bankrupt and the sewer system we use a lot of water and so our sewer rates were outrageous.

We had a consultant that the gas company provided to look at our power costs, gas costs and water costs and to see what we could do to save money.

He was just flabbergasted to see how high our water and sewer was. Just because of the county we are in. If we were in a different county, we would not have that. Because of the financial mess Jefferson County is in, our sewer and water costs tripled, 360% over the last five years, and you cannot pass that on to consumers.

– *Wayne Pate*

Continuing challenges

Looking ahead the sewer is a continuing problem and health care will continue to raise its ugly head; how the government will address those issues is related to our products.

People talk about putting an extra tax on snack food.

We also face obesity issues, salt, acrylamide issues...

Trans fat was an obesity issue. We used to cook in non-trans fat oil years ago. We had no trans fat in our chips. Then the soybean lobby said tropical oils were bad even though many doctors felt coconut oils and other oils were the best oils.

So we had to move away from tropical oils because they

were considered evil and we moved to hydrogenated soybean oil because that gave us the shelf life and stability. And the soybean people pushed that by having laws passed that discouraged the importation of tropical oil.

But now it has gone the other way and we are back in non-trans fat oil, tropical oils, being very careful not to change the price of our product. And we are always prepared with different blends of oils that we can use to keep that bag of chips at 99 cents.

And it changes day to day about what is good and what is bad for you. When you were a kid you ate butter, but that became evil and you were supposed to eat margarine. But now you are supposed to eat butter again because margarine is evil because it has trans fat in it.

We have to constantly keep adjusting to address what the government says is bad.

Now, we have low-fat and no-fat type snacks, but they don't sell very well. People lie, they say, "I eat that kind of stuff," but they lie.

We say there are no junk foods, there are only junk food diets. Eat everything in moderation. No, don't eat a five ounce bag of potato chips for every meal. Yeah, we have to address those government issues of saying it's evil.

But is it is not evil, a bag of chips won't kill you. Go out and play some, eat a Snicker bar once in a while, it is not going to hurt you.

–*Mark McCutcheon*

Government regulations

Government regulations? We are inspected by USDA, FDA, state health, local health, EPA, OSHA...

But we have a philosophy about all this regulation. Our desire is to be better than any regulation would require us to be. For sanitation, for every facet in our organization. We want to be better. We contract with a company who inspects us; it takes three days or more, their requirements are stricter than the government's and we are more thoroughly inspected by them than any government agency.

So when we get inspected by any government agency in any area, we know, because of own inspections, we have even exceeded the government's requirements.

We sell to PXs, commissaries on military bases, ships' stores, and anytime you sell to the government in any form or fashion – prisons, we sell to prisons, all of that – you get into complete contract compliance, and OSHA covers everything.

The local health people check us periodically, the state heath people check us periodically, USDI Pork Standards, USDA, and we get inspected because of the pork rinds we make, just like we are a slaughterhouse.

But you need to set standards for yourself that are higher than any regulatory agency.

– *Wayne Pate*

Lesson Three

Some Basic Economics and Administrative

Stuff You Need To Know

Chapter 12

Thinking like an accountant

There is no business like show business, but there are several businesses like accounting.
– David Letterman

Introduction: Okay, we have discussed factors, from cancer to sewers, from regulations to lobbying, that can impact business. Now for the fun stuff. The basics of economics. I know you can't wait to get started, so here we go.

The four factors of production

To be basically literate in economics, it is important to know the four factors of production. The four factors are: natural resources, capital, labor and entrepreneurship. Each of these factors contributes to any product being made. And every company, just to stay in business, must carefully control the costs of each of these factors.

Natural resources include land, water, trees, minerals – things that basically include the earth.

Capital includes tools, machines, and anything else that a business uses to produce their goods or services. Without capital the company would not be able to produce anything.

The third factor of production is labor which includes everybody that works in the company from the factory workers to the owner of the company.

The final factor is entrepreneurship. Entrepreneurs are the people that start their own business, taking all the necessary risks in order to, hopefully, make a profit. Without these people and their ideas, no companies would ever start. As the famed management guru, Peter Drucker, once noted, "Whenever you see a successful business, someone once made a courageous decision."

Looking at Golden Flake, the natural resources are potatoes, the capital is all the equipment they use to make chips, the labor is anyone who works for Golden Flake and the entrepreneurs were Mose Lischkoff and Frank Mosher who, in 1923, started making chips in the basement of a local grocery store.

The four factors are intriguing because they represent, in simple form, how complicated our economy can be. When you look at chips, or any other manufactured product, you must understand how our economy is so interconnected, how so many factors must click and work together, just to get a bag of chips on the grocery store shelf. And we touched upon that earlier by detailing just what it takes to get a potato to the Golden Flake factory and how many things can go wrong with a simple potato crop.

You got to appreciate what we have

Which brings us to the next point. We have a very sophisticated system in place just to make a potato chip. But when other companies – we are going to depart from Golden Flake for a moment here –when other companies go to foreign lands, they have to build up an entire agricultural system just to get chips into any grocery store.

Consider what Frito-Lay had to do in parts of Asia, just to put a system in place just to provide potatoes to make chips. It is no secret that one of Frito-Lay's biggest selling products is Lays potato chips. But in 2008, because the four factors of production did not mesh together, Frito-Lay could not make enough Lays potato chips to meet the demand for them in Asia. This cost Frito-Lay millions of dollars.

So Frito-Lay had to start putting the four factors in place. What we take for granted in America, a smooth operating system to grow potatoes, ship them to Golden Flake, manufacture the chips and sent them to market, did not exist in parts of Asia.

Just to ensure that it would always have potatoes, Frito-Lay gave farmers seeds and tractors. Then it had to buy irrigation and water management systems for the farmers.

To get the millions of potatoes it needed, Frito-Lay had to work with more than 10,000 farmers working in over 12,000 acres across Punjab, UP, Karnataka, Jharkhand, West Bengal, Kashmir and Maharashtra.

Frito-Lay also had to introduce 'tougher potatoes'. In 2008, it faced a potato shortage due to crop failure in Maharashtra on account of drought, in Karnataka due to late blight and in Punjab due to frost. These losses could have been avoided by 'tougher potatoes'.

So Frito-Lay introduced six high-quality, high-yield potato varieties to the farmers.

The point of this little Frito-Lay story? Note all the factors that we already have in place in America to ensure that you can eat all the Golden Flake chips you want. We have a very sophisticated infrastructure system which we take for granted.

And any economic system, even if it wants to do something as simple as put an affordable bag of potato chips on the shelf, must have a reliable system in place that can supply the most basic of materials, in this case potatoes.

Frito-Lay had to build that entire system in some Asian companies just to produce a bag of chips.

A cardinal rule of economics is proven once again. Never take anything for granted. Even a simple bag of potato chips.

Cost Structure (I)

Quote: If the cost structure of any business is too high – end of story.

– *Anon*

In economics, the term 'cost structure' underlies the thinking of every businessman or woman.

Perhaps the best way to understand cost structure is to look at the potato farmer who supplies Golden Flake with potatoes. It is important that the farmer sell his raw materials (potatoes) at a high enough price to cover his costs and ensure a profit. But he can't sell his potatoes too high; Golden Flake will go somewhere else.

The basic problem any potato farmer faces is this: What may be the right price today may be too low tomorrow because of changing market conditions.

The farmer therefore, in economics speak, "has to analyze his cost structures very carefully, so that his expenses, i.e. his production costs (wages for workers, fertilizer, water, transport to the factory, etc.), do not exceed his income."

In short, potatoes just don't show up at the Golden Flake factory. And the farmer who grows them cannot afford to be some hayseed chewing on a straw, hitching up his pants and sticking a finger in the air to see which way the wind is blowing.

He has many things to contend with: the weather, crop prices and, perhaps scariest of all, the federal government. How scary? Here is a government handout aimed at simplifying the farmer's bookkeeping.

All costs will not have the same allocation percentages. Also, some expenses will be easier to allocate then others. Use farm records when available and when they are not available, use your best estimate. In the last row (row 31), there are cells to enter the number of acres of potatoes planted each year. These acreages are used to calculate the "3-Year Average Per Acre Cost" (Column I). Finally, two of the expense lines, Depreciation and Interest, are grayed out. This is because the Schedule F value of these expenses is for tax purposes, which differ from economic depreciation and economic interest. These costs will be accounted for on the Capital sheet.

Hmm – okay – and now you know why Ronald Reagan said the scariest phrase in the world is: "I am from the federal government and I am here to help you."

But to return to our main point. The farmer, like every other supplier of Golden Flake, is a business owner and has expenses he must meet. Here is a quick list of expenses that farmers face:

Car & Truck
Chemicals
Conservation Expenses
Depreciation
Customer Hire
Employee Program Benefits
Feed
Fertilizers & Lime
Freight & Trucking
Gasoline, Fuel & Oil
Insurance
Interest
Labor Hired
Pension and Profit Sharing
Rental & Leases
Repairs & Maintenance
Seeds, Plants
Storage & Warehousing
Supplies Purchased
Taxes
Utilities
Office Expense
Legal & Professional Fees
Marketing Expenses

In short farming ain't cheap. In fact major capital expenditures include: machinery, irrigation and drainage, building facilities for storage and handling, vehicles, and on farm washing/grading/ packaging equipment.

These costs add up. For a 100-acre potato farm, these expenses can run over $550,000 a year.

And beyond the money you need to invest in equipment (capital expenses), you have operating expenses. The most significant direct operating expenses are incurred in washing, grading, packaging, and marketing the product.

But wait, the farmer faces other direct expenses including seed, fertilizer, crop protection, labor and machinery maintenance.

Farm machinery ain't cheap

As we have discovered, there are layers upon layers of complicity in every aspect of the potato chip production process. Let's look at a simple tractor. A new one will cost a farmer about $110,000. And that tractor keeps costing him. He has to pay interest on the loan he took out to buy the tractor, he has to pay insurance on it, he has to depreciate it on his income tax, he has to build a machine shed to shelter it, he has repairs on it, he has yearly maintenance, he has to buy fuel to run it, he has lubrication costs, and he has to pay an operator to run the tractor. Remember that when you pay labor, there are also costs of labor including base wage, FICA, and insurance.

The farmer also has to consider dependability costs. If the tractor breaks down, sure you have the repair cost, but you have other costs as well. If you can't harvest the potatoes at the right time, crop yield and quality losses might occur.

Cost Structure (II)

Which all gets us back to our main point. The farmer represents the average businessperson who has a lot of expenses. These expenses represent his 'cost structure', and unless he has a very good handle on what his expenses are and what he needs do to make a profit, he can't even begin to price his potatoes when

Golden Flake comes calling.

But a firm understanding of what it costs him to grow those potatoes, a complete understanding of ALL his expenses will keep him in business and Golden Flake in potatoes.

Cost of Sales and General and Administrative Expenses

Quote: The great thing about working in the accounting department is that everybody counts.

– *Anon*

Let's talk about accounting. Don't worry, we won't throw a lot of terms at you. If fact we hope that you will see that accounting is not a mystical science, but rather can be explained in simple everyday terms. But then if your accountant did that, he couldn't charge $400 to prepare your tax return.

First, let's consider why it is so important for Golden Flake to watch two types of expenses. The first is Cost of Sales. The other types of expenses include Selling, General and Administrative Expenses, also known as SGA expenses.

Let's look a little closer at what Cost of Sales expenses are. Cost of Sales are the costs that go into creating the snack products that Golden Flake sells.

The key concept is Cost of Sales only INCLUDE what is needed to produce a potato chip.

For example, the Cost of Sales for a bag of Golden Flake Chips might include the cost of the potatoes and seasonings used, the costs of running the machine to manufacture the product and the cost of the bag the chips go into.

But the costs of sending the chips to stores and the cost of the salespeople and the route people would be excluded from the Cost of Sales expenses. Costs of Sales only include WHAT it took to make the product.

Selling, General and Administrative Expenses

All the other expenses involved in selling, marketing, bookkeeping, shipping, heck I could on and on, but the point is, all the other expenses that a company incurs are thrown in the SGA category. This includes the person at the front desk, the gas for the trucks, the light and heat for the offices – heck SGA covers everything.

Okay so what?

Well, as we discussed in a previous chapter, a lot of things can happen to drive the costs of potatoes up. And Golden Flake can't do a lot about that.

But good management at any company, be it Golden Flake or Ted's Tire Repair, can control the SGA expenses. You can look at a company's SGA expenses and see if management is doing a good job. If SGA expenses are eating up 75% of a company's profits, something is wrong. Somebody in management is not watching the ship. However, if you compare Golden Flake and its competitors and SGA is about the same percent for all of them, say 50% of revenue, then somebody is keeping a close watch on expenses.

In short, a good management team will often attempt to keep SGA expenses under tight control and limited to a certain percentage of revenue by reducing corporate overhead (i.e. cost cutting, employee lay-offs).

Having said all of that, let's take a look at Golden Flake's position in the snack world.

We must realize that Golden Flake has little if any control over what they can sell a bag of chips for. Golden Flake is a relatively small player in a big market.

Consider these numbers. The total revenue of the savory snack food industry is about $60 billion a year. Golden Flake's total revenue was $108.34 million which is minor when compared to Frito-Lay who has a stronghold on the top position in the market. Frito-Lay has total revenues of about $45.3 billion a year and keeps upping its market share; once it controlled about 40% of the snack market. Now, Frito-Lay controls over 50% of the market share. Again, compared to Frito-Lay, which Golden Flake executives call the "Evil Empire", Golden Flake does not even hold a market share of 1%.

Why is this important?

If you are hanging onto a small market segment and if the Evil Empire is trying to take over the kingdom of snack foods, you better watch every dime you spend. Dollars do not come to Golden Flake easily and they must beware of every dime they spend.

And even in the best run companies, like Golden Flake, expenses will eat you up. Let's look at some actual Golden Flake numbers.

In one quarter they sell about $28 million of snack foods. Hey, that's not bad. Let's take the money and run.

Whoops – remember the Cost of Sales. How much did it cost Golden Flake to produce all those snack foods? About $15 million.

Ouch. Well it is not anyone's fault, but it takes money to make a product. So out of that $28 million we made selling chips, take away $15 million. Hmm that leaves us with a profit of $13 million. I can live with that.

Whoops. Again! What about the lights and heats and trucks and gas and salaries and benefits and salespeople and route people and executives and workers and advertising and marketing and...

Oh yes, those sales, and general and administrative expenses, the costs of doing business. That costs Golden Flake about $12 million a quarter.

So out of that $28 million worth of chips we take away the $15 million in Cost of Sales and the $12 million in SGA expenses and we have about a one million dollar profit. And remember we have not even discussed how many taxes will be taken out of that.

A Quick Aside: How far will some snack food companies go to cut administrative expenses?

As we continue our joy ride through potato chip country, we have been learning about how the economy really works, from how scientific illiteracy – think acrylamides – can cost a company millions, to how something as simple as growing potatoes can go terribly wrong, due to a number of factors.

And this is a very short lesson in how outsourcing affects all areas of our economy, even the potato chip world.

And that statement, initially, seems to make no sense. How can anyone outsource chips which are made in America? In fact I often hear people say stuff like, "I try to 'buy American' whenever I can, but the only things that I can buy that are 'made in America' are Potato Chips and Soda." True, making and then packaging potato chips and bottling soda have not been outsourced to foreign countries.

So, the actual making of the chips has not been outsourced and Golden Flake does not outsource any jobs, but the outsourcing trend is starting to hit the snack food industry.

And it makes sense. Think back on administrative expenses. Every time Golden Flake sells a bag of chips, a portion of that sale must go to pay for bookkeepers and accountants and others in the office who must keep up with the paperwork. And if you are a stockholder, wouldn't you like that money to go to you, wouldn't you like to receive a bigger dividend check every quarter?

And that takes us back to a simple economics principle. If Golden Flake earns a dollar and 25 cents of that dollar goes to office staff, that is 25 cents that cannot be listed as profit and pay shareholders.

But why do you need an accountant sitting in Birmingham, Alabama? After all numbers are numbers, and I can pay an accountant in India a lot less than I pay you to sit in my office and crunch numbers.

Of course, Golden Flake has no plans to replace its office staff with cheaper Indian labor, but other snack companies are buying into the trend of outsourcing 'administrative functions'.

One example, McCain Foods in Canada axed 25 jobs in New Brunswick as part of a move to outsource accounting functions to India. These jobs cover the day-to-day accounting activities, such as paying invoices, tracking costs and general accounting functions.

And company executives noted that English is an official language in India, so they're able to communicate back and forth.

Plus McCain officials noted that India has a tremendous IT infrastructure making it easy to communicate with people.

And McCain officials are right. Financial services and accounting represents a growing opportunity for India and a growing opportunity for American companies to cut costs.

Fred Schaeffer, president and CEO of McCain Foods (Canada), said that his company was moving towards outsourcing in order to "level the playing field" with other multinational firms who have already taken similar action.

"In this rapidly-changing, dynamic marketplace, it is imperative that we do whatever is necessary to help us remain competitive," Schaeffer said in a press release.

"Engaging a third party to manage some of our financial activities such as paying invoices and tracking costs will significantly improve our competitiveness."

The True Cost of Hiring You: A short lesson in labor economics

Quote: Recently, I was asked if I was going to fire an employee who made a mistake that cost the company $600,000. No, I replied, I just spent $600,000 training him. Why would I want somebody to hire his experience?

– *Thomas Watson*

A key concept in any economics discussion is labor. You are the labor when you work for someone. You may be deemed 'an employee', but in economics terms, you are 'the cost of labor'. And to understand the true cost of labor, you must look at what Golden Flake and other companies truly pay for an employee.

To be an effective economics thinker, you cannot think as an 'employee'. Escape that mindset and think like a CEO. To top management you are 'labor' and there are costs to hiring you that reach far beyond your salary.

For example, when Golden Flake hires an employee, the true cost of an employee is the employee's hourly rate plus an additional cost representing 56.55% of the wage rate. In other words, if you get paid an hourly rate $10.00 you are really costing Golden Flake at least $15.66.

This additional cost increases every time Golden Flake faces health insurance increases and every time the federal government imposes new regulations and various employment taxes.

Let's look at an example. You are paid $10 an hour and you get paid $400 a week. But as a $400.00-a-week employee you really cost Golden Flake $626.20 a week.

These additional costs include:

Mandatory Costs (required by law)
Federal Social Security Tax 7.65%
Federal Unemployment Tax 0.80%
State Unemployment Tax 2.9%
Worker's Compensation 4.3%
Total Mandatory Cost 15.65%

Hiring Costs (costs involved in putting an employee into the payroll system)
Recruiting, hiring, training, bookkeeping, payroll 6.90%
Severance Pay 0.10%
Total Hiring Cost 7.00%

Discretionary Costs (costs which by practice have in most instances become obligatory)

Vacation 4.90%

Holidays 3.40%

Sick Pay 1.30%

Pension Plan 5.40%

Profit Sharing 1.20%

Health & Life Insurance 11.9%

Bonuses & Incentives 0.40%

Contribute to Thrift Plan 0.60%

Non-Working Time 3.50%

Miscellaneous Benefits 1.30%

Total Discretionary Costs 33.9%

TOTAL ADDITIONAL COSTS 56.55%

The Real World of Golden Flake

Two and two makes four.

I was Chairman of the Board of Trustees at Baptist Health Systems and I have been on the board about 27, 28 years. And Health South was a competitor and we would look at their numbers and say something is not right. We are in the health care business and how are they able to do this; we are unable to do that. Well they weren't. They were falsifying the numbers.

Well, we have seen companies in the snack business that were doing things that we would say we couldn't do. And we knew that we were way more efficient than they are. They can't long do it, but they will keep on doing it, but they can't survive. One day – Chapter 11.

Listen, two and two makes four. Doesn't make eight or six. It's just four. And you got to make the numbers come out.

We make two to three cents on the sale of each product.

– *Wayne Pate*

Show me the money

From a shareholder perspective – they don't care how many bags of chips we produce a day, they just get that bottom line, earnings and dividends.

Our senior management team gets down to basics regarding numbers, in dollars in revenues, in sales.

And we know how many chips have got to go out that door, how busy we must keep production. We look at certain margins we must hit based on the purchasing of ingredients – the salt and potatoes and corn and oil and...

Well you get the picture. We got to produce that product as cheaply as we can. We have to keep the costs of goods manufactured under control.

And then we have to worry about General Administrative Expenses. And then what it costs us to get the product to the stores; how much does it cost in delivery? And watch how much we spend in promotion and advertising, and health insurance and advertising and lawyers. And that's just a few things under Administrative Expenses.

And then you put all the expenses in a cup and shake it up; it will show you how you did that month in earnings and stuff.

And some months you can have a blip, where it is tough to make earnings. For instance, lately production has been fighting high costs; we all have been on both sides, from fuel that has jumped up like crazy to cooking oil and the cost of corn because our government thinks we need ethanol.

– *Mark McCutcheon*

Cutting Distribution Costs

Transportation costs can be high, as gas goes up and up; it can eat into any profits you have. So we keep looking for ways to slice our transportation costs. We go to every store in Birmingham, so we said, "Why not deliver for other people too?"

We have picked up some what we call partner brands. Buzz's Best Cookies had independent distributors in town. So we started putting their cookies on our trucks.

The thought process is centered around our route people. How do I make a route person be efficient, how do I make his stop more valuable to him, so that he is putting more merchandise in and making more money?

And the answer is – let's choose items that are on that truck so that you, as a route person, can become more valuable to that store.

Now our route person is delivering a top line of cookies as well as Golden Flake potato chips. That lets you stay longer on that stop because you are putting up more money on that stop. I have less stops, I am driving less mileage, but I am making more money. Rather than driving 500 miles a week, I am driving 300.

But we want the most profitable items on our trucks, because we are a direct store delivery system. Sure, everybody wants their products on our trucks; we are going there anyway, we might as well carry their product.

But if it is a low margin item, we don't want that because you are taking your time and effort dealing with this low margin item, bubble gum, pick anything rather than selling potato chips and stuff. We are very careful about what we allow in the trucks.

But our route driver becomes more valuable in that store because of the items he is carrying. Instead of just hitting 12 feet of space at the grocery store, he is now covering 24 feet. He is more valuable to that store manager now, because it is not, "Oh yeah you only have that 12 feet, we will get to you soon." It becomes, "No, we need you here, you have all these items that my customer needs."

So we have try to pick the right partner brands that means we are more valuable to the store and it's more money for us and that route person too.

– Mark McCutcheon

Making everything count

We were recycling before recycling was cool, even trying to make gasohol. You know how that worked out.

But we provide the starch that might be in your shirt right now; that could be our potato starch. We send our potato peelings to cattle feed.

We guarantee that if the food gets stale in your grocery store, we will pick it up and all that stale food comes back here and floor sweepings and any bad product goes on a trailer and it goes up to Central Alabama and it is made into chicken feed additive.

We use cardboard boxes for our routes. It is not a one-way trip; it is six to ten trips for cardboard boxes, then they go to cardboard recycling. The only thing we are not able to recycle at this point is the actual flexible bag that the product is in because it is a combination of materials and the manufacturers of the bags have not figured out how to melt and make park benches, fence posts out of it.

We are even looking at a project now; we are recycling our water. We are looking at a total recycle of water to drinking level; that is on the drawing board, that would be less water going down the sewer line.

That would be a capital investment of over 4 million dollars.

But you look at every way you can cut costs.

Get the right potato peelers and you can increase finished chip production by 5 to 6% with no jump in potato usage. You can use 6 to 8% fewer pounds of potatoes. More efficient peeling will also improved finished chip quality, lowered maintenance and cleaning costs, and reduce the quantity of chip scraps entering packages.

And that is just by having the right peelers.

– David Jones

Reducing packaging waste

On our end, we have programs in place to reduce packaging waste. That is part of the four million we spent on new equipment. In some items, the small bags, it is extremely difficult to make them small and still have enough head space for the nitrogen to preserve the chips. There is more scrap in the small bags than the big bags.

We were running in excess of 10% of scrap in packaging potato chips. Then we put the new machines in and we have been at less than 2.5% waste and have been as low as 1.5%. We have drastically reduced the number of bad bags we have produced and that helps us too, because we need more good bags and fewer bad bags.

– David Jones

Those important but expensive employees

Employees need to know that it costs Golden Flake more to hire them than just their paychecks. They need to know that we are concerned with their financial well-being from a personal standpoint too; we want to make sure they have benefits they can afford, provide them with decent health care. And that is a cost of employing them.

A single employee on our health plan a week pays about $20 dollars a week, and in the meetings we talk about the ratio, the employee pays 30%, we pay 70%.

In one employee meeting, I talked about an article I just read the other day; nationally a single employee getting what the newspaper said was a decent health care plan pays about $60 a week. So our employees pay a lot less, because we cover it for them. But that is an expense of employing them.

When you need to cut costs in one area, because costs are

increasing in another, you look everywhere. It can get down to health care. When I first came here, we paid for the employees' health insurance. It was cheap; we paid for 100% of the employee and their families.

That meant we had every Tom and Dick's illegitimate child on our health insurance. The employee thinks, "Why would I go put it on my wife's health insurance and have to pay? I am going to put it on Golden Flake."

Well when health care costs started to go up, we went, "Wait a minute, we have got to see if the wife has some health insurance coverage. We have to see if it really is their wife, their child. We have to double-check. Health insurance is not so cheap anymore; we have to be sure that the ones we cover are getting effective coverage."

And we have to be fair, ask tough questions. In the health coverage we have, how do we balance someone who packs potato chips in a box and they are not making $300,000 a year? How do we make it so we can give them good quality health care, what they can afford and what we can afford to help pay?

It is really a balancing act there trying to figure that out, but a lot of companies don't take the time to be fair.

We are a good company; I was going to work here a year until I got a real job.

Because our predecessors cared about everyone in this company and we are charged with carrying that on. As stewards of this company, we must think about how to pass this company onto the next generation, not think, "What is in it for me."

But that's the way corporate America is now looked at: "Heck, I have my Golden Parachute; heck, I am gone." That is not the way we look at it.

The question we have asked for years is not: "How does it affect the company?" Rather, when something is about to change, if it is the health insurance, anything, we ask, "How will this affect the employees, who are also some of our stockholders, who are also consumers?"

It is a balancing act. I will stick with health care. How many benefits do we give? What do we ask them to pay for that benefit, knowing we cannot raise the price of our product just to cover that benefit?

In a potato crisis you certainly can't go out there for three weeks and raise the prices; you just have to grin and bear it and try to work through it.

Our health care has increased over 20% at least in just a few years.

You try to find ways to spread the cost of the health insurance around where it will not be a major disruptive force on your earnings or your employees.

You have to make adjustments. And so you make adjustments to the health care plan to make it a win-win situation for the employee and the company. Plus you educate your employees; we have employees that use the emergence room as a regular doctor. Through the use of dollars, you have to force people to do things.

Like I said, a lot of people use the emergency room as their doctor, well never for me, because I don't want to spend six hours in there because they will take the heart attack guy before they take someone with a cold.

We are trying to say to our employees, just go to the Doc in the Box, it's cheaper.

How do you force them out of the bad habits that raise everyone's health care costs? You say, "If you go to the emergency room and you are not admitted to the hospital – if you are having a heart attack by all means go to the hospital – but if you are going there because you have a headache or the flu your co-pay is going to be outrageous."

– *Mark McCutcheon*

Lesson Four

Neat Financial Terms

Chapter 13

It's More than a Bag of Chips. It's Stocks and Bonds and Capital Expenditures and Inelastic and Demand and Other Neat Financial Terms. Plus LIBOR!!!

Remind people that profit is the difference between revenue and expense. This makes you look smart.
– Scott Adams

Introduction: This section will clearly explain stocks and bonds, and walk through Golden Flake's financial statements explaining such terms as stockholder equity, dividends, preferred and common stocks, bonds. And how stocks (sometimes) pay for capital expenditures.

We made a deal with you when we wrote this book. We would teach you about economics and terms like stock and bonds and equity and discombobulate, by using The Real World of Golden Flake as an example. Okay, we didn't agree to teach you the meaning of discombobulate, it's just a fun word to say.

Let's start with a basic overview of stocks and bonds by following the growth of Golden Flake.

In 1923, Mose Lischkoff and Frank Mosher had a simple idea which grew into Golden Flake, which hires over 1200 employees a year and cooks over 100 million pounds of potato a year.

But they started small and cooked potato chips in the basement of a grocery store. Soon they had two salesmen working for them and had more and more customers.

Now if you are Mose and Frank, you need capital, a term which means money. You need money to buy equipment and a building and to pay employees or else your business will not grow. Let's face it; you can only make so much money selling chips out of a basement.

Where do you get this money? You can take the money you make from selling potato chips and put it in a savings account and when you have a million dollars or more, you can go build a potato chip factory. Hmm, that might take a while, because after you pay for the raw materials and cooking oil and employees and rent on the basement and packaging and employees, well you just don't have that much money left over.

And if you wait around for that savings account to grow, a competitor might move in, build a factory and put you out of business. It is a cruel world. Another idea, go to your mother-in-law and ask her for a loan. That is assuming that you married into a rich family and you have a nice mother-in-law.

Another option? Go to a bank and ask for a million dollars.

Or you can sell shares in the company? What?

You can get some friends together and say, I will give a percent of my company, if you give me some money. And 20 friends give you money and they own part of the company.

That, by the way, is what a stock is. You buy a stock and you buy part of a company. The more stocks you buy, the more of the company you own. If you have a lot of money, you can buy over 50% of the company and control the company.

In short, stocks are shares in a company or corporation. When a privately owned company, Golden Flake (just Mose and his partner Frank own the company), wants to become publicly owned, Golden Flake issues stocks which you buy to own part of Golden Flake.

Those shares are then bought and sold on the stock exchange.

Fair enough, but how do you make money on your stock in Golden Flake. The basic idea behind the stock market is Golden Flake will make more and more money and someone wants a piece of this great company. So you sell them your stock in Golden Flake for more than you paid for it.

Therefore, if you bought a share of Golden Flake for $5 today, you expect that share will be worth more in the future, at which point you can sell the share and make lots of money. The risk is that Golden Flake or any company may not gain value over time, in which case you lose money. Additionally, Golden Flake will pay you dividends. If Golden Flake makes a profit, they will share a part of that profit with you. You will get a dividend or 'profit check' in the mail four times a year.

Of course, Golden Flake may need to put its profit back into buying a new machine that cooks potato chip, so you may not get a dividend that year. The amount of dividend you get is determined by the board of directors, the people you and the other stockholders have elected to oversee the company.

Bonds are relatively simple as well – they're just loans by another name. Think of a bond as a mortgage on your house. The bank is pleased to give you a loan for your house, because they know they can always sell your house to collect on your loan.

If Golden Flake wants to build a new storage shed (capital expenditure) to store potatoes, Golden Flake may issue bonds and, like a mortgage, agree to pay back the amount borrowed plus a certain amount of interest (also known as a coupon) by a certain date. When an investor buys a bond, he or she is lending money to the seller, and then makes a profit on the interest.

Finally, a bit of trivia.

In the Middle Ages, the Catholic Church did not approve of paying interest on borrowed money. Neither did the Muslim and Jewish religions. Yet borrowers needing money would go to lenders and compensate the lenders for the temporary use of their money.

But what could they call this compensation? Since the Church did not allow the payment, there could be no word for it. Instead, it was called the money that 'is between' (borrowing and repayment). Since Latin was the business language over all Europe, they would say *"inter est"* meaning 'is between'. And thus a new word was coined.

Just thought you'd like to know.

The Real World of Golden Flake
The cost of being a publically traded company:

What does being a publically traded company have to do with the cost of a bag of chips? It adds on costs that we cannot really pass on to the customer.

There are regulations and more regulations we must meet. We must comply with all the Security and Exchange Commission's regulations; we must conduct numerous audits. And then there are, of course, all of the annual reports and quarterly reports – 10-Ks, 10-Qs, annual reports, interim reports and the dividends and annual meeting costs.

We are so closely held, we don't do dog and pony shows around the country. We have one stockholder who has 58% of the stock.

In fact, you can argue that a company our size should not be public. When Golden Flake went public years ago, that was the thing to do; it was relatively cheap in those days.

Now with Sarbanes-Oxley and all the new regulations and costs associated with them, many companies our size are going private and many companies our size look at the SOX regulations and say, "Heck, we would be crazy to go public."

With SOX, the pendulum on costs went crazy, but that has been fixed to a certain extent now that they are treating us as a smaller company. It's reasonable, but we just have to be very careful what information we put out there to inform our stockholders, but not inform our competitors.

There is a real balance between reporting what is necessary and still not giving away any competitive information.

It costs us at least half a million a year, that is administrative costs alone, to be a publically traded company. That includes legal expenses, extra accounting costs, extra personnel, the cost of publishing the reports, proxy solicitations to get the stockholders to vote to report at the stockholder meeting so we have a quorum.

– *Patty Townsend*

Capital expenditures and the importance of 'payback'

We have capital expenditures that we look at; and based on the company's need, we look out five years, and say we need to invest in a new potato peeler.

We call it a wish list, capital expenditures, what we want to do and what we got to do.

We just put a new roof on the building; we just finished that – that is a got to do. You have to stay dry. But there is no payback on a new roof.

A lot of our equipment has payback; a couple of years ago, we looked at our equipment. We really don't have debt; that is one thing that helps us. But it was time to upgrade the equipment to become more productive.

We took out a pretty big loan for us, $4 million; for others it is pocket change. Companies our size seem to love debt, and it is taking some of them down too. We finally found technology in packing machines that makes the bags and puts the product in. The technology had reached a level, that it would streamline our production process, makes us more efficient and productive. It was a good payback.

The technology had reached such a level where we said we should really enlist in this project, conveyer systems and packaging machines, and it really had a payback. It helped us control our costs and be more productive. It helped us not waste seasoning and packing film. Plus we could get the work done with fewer workers, which saved labor costs.

We did not have a layoff; we had lost some people through attrition, they retired, went to another job, and we used a temporary service for a while, to fill in for those people. But we were able to save the jobs of the people at the plant, even though we went from 36 packaging machines in these areas to nine.

– *Mark McCutcheon*

Financing the machines

The new equipment cost us $4 million and we paid the loan back in about four years.

We paid the loan back but the payback was targeted for almost three. In fact if we can do a payback in less than three, we think it is wonderful and we did this payback in less than a year and a half.

On the packaging equipment we had a loan, LIBOR plus 1.75, which was very favorable, and at the time, the interest level was very low.

LIBOR is the inter-bank rate set by trading with London and New York overnight; every morning when you watch CNBC they almost always have LIBOR.

We had great timing. Now, especially in this economic crisis, LIBOR is way up; especially because of the crisis, none of the banks are loaning to each, the interest rate is extremely high.

We were able to get a loan at about 3%; we rapidly paid it off which is the philosophy of this company to be debt free and every opportunity we paid extra payments on that and paid it off ahead of schedule.

We believe in using operating cash; we do not believe in issuing stock to raise money. We have not issued new stock in the 20 years I have been here.

You have to look at all your options, look at your rate, look at your payback; you just don't jump into a fixed rate. We went with LIBOR; it was more favorable and trends showed that we could save money with LIBOR compared to a fixed rate.

– *Patty Townsend*

Chapter 14

Terms Necessary to Understanding the World of Economics

Without continual growth and progress, such words as improvement, achievement, and success have no meaning.
– Benjamin Franklin

Introduction: This section will cover terms you should have learned somewhere in college or high school if you were paying attention. These terms impact The Real World of Golden Flake and determine how much it can charge for a bag of chips. But – WARNING – the first part of the chapter deals with the academic world of supply and demand. How they teach it in the classroom. The second half of the chapter – The Real World of Golden Flake – tells it 'the way it is' and how 'supply and demand' is determined by shelf space and the 'Snack Food Wars'. And it also talks about how Golden Flake looks at the costs and benefits before introducing a new product.

Costs and Benefits

Remember, we discussed Costs and Benefits earlier when we were talking about packaging. How good does a package have to be, and when does it get ridiculous to build too good of a package?

We have limited time and money and we must decide the best way to spend that time and money. Golden Flake is the same way. It does not have an unlimited supply of money – it can only spend the money that it earns through selling chips.

What is the best way to spend that money? Invest in new machines that can reduce the cost of making potato chips, invest in training employees so they will be more productive, invest in commercials to sell more chips, invest in delivery trucks that use less gas, invest in introducing new products to the market, give more money back to their shareholders – the choices go on and on.

The same theory of limited resources applies to you. You must make decisions. Which uses of your limited resources are best? Which uses generate the most value? You have made a choice to read this book and that is a great decision! (Okay, we might be slightly biased.) But why have you made the decision to read this book? Well, you live in a market economy and you must understand how the economy works. If you play a game, you must know the rules.

But this book is costing you time. You just kissed half an hour good-bye and you will never get that half hour back.

In short, if you are the CEO of Golden Flake or any company, it boils down to – **warning – important economics term ahead** – costs and benefits. Every decision Golden Flake makes or you make involves costs and benefits.

Costs and benefits change behavior

Consumers, Golden Flake customers, change their buying habits when their expected costs and benefits change. Very few Golden Flake customers decide, for no reason at all, to stop buying potato chips or to start buying ten more bags a month. The costs and benefits of buying potato chips will determine their behavior.

In other words if a bag of Golden Flake chips doubles in price is there any more benefit to buying that bag? The cost may be too high, and you can benefit yourself better by buying two bags of Frito-Lay chips at a much lower price.

This concept of costs and benefits drives Golden Flake's behavior. Golden Flake will weigh costs and benefits before sticking a price on a bag of chips or launching a new product. And you will weigh costs and benefits before buying a bag of Golden Flake chips.

Demand

If the benefits to buying Golden Flake chips outweigh the cost, you will buy a bag or two. You will increase the demand for Golden Flake.

Note how we casually snuck that word in. Demand. Economists use the term *demand* to indicate *willingness to buy*. Your choice to buy Golden Flake depends upon many factors. Heck, Jay Leno is coming on television and you have a burning desire for chips and you can walk to the store and back in ten minutes, why not buy some chips.

But besides late night hunger, it also depends on how much money you have in your wallet. In other words, price – what are those chips going to cost?

Of course, the price of Golden Flake chips is not the only reason consumers buy them:

1. They just plain like the taste of Golden Flake compared to other chips.
2. Consumers' income level. Sure chips are cheap, but buy five bags a week, that is over ten bucks a week, which is over $40 a month, which is close to $500 a year.
3. The prices of substitute and complementary goods. In other words, why buy Golden Flake at two bucks a bag, when you can buy Snickers for 65 cents. They will both satisfy your hunger.
4. The number of consumers in the market for Golden Flake: if there are 100 people demanding Golden Flake chips and there are only 50 bags, Golden Flake can charge more. Unlikely, but it can happen.

Demand and supply shifters

The reasons listed above are *demand shifters*. If any of them changes, the demand for Golden Flake chips may *shift*. For example, new research indicates that eating Golden Flake chips and only Golden Flake chips will increase your IQ by 30 points. Hey, that's a no-brainer (sorry for the bad pun). This IQ research will give Golden Flake chips scores of new customers and may even change what Golden Flake can charge for their chips.

Okay we have discussed demand. The other side of demand is Supply, which indicates *willingness to sell*.

In other words, how many chips is Golden Flake willing to sell? Like demand, the supply of how many chips Golden Flake makes depends upon several factors. This may not come as news, but price is a main factor. For example, Golden Flake might be happy to sell 1,000 bags of chips at $3 a bag, but would be delighted to sell 2,000 bags at $4 a bag. But at 50 cents a bag, Golden Flake doesn't want to sell any chips. Why sell your product at a loss?

Golden Flake might be willing to sell more chips for other reasons. These include:

1. Cost of inputs – hey the price of potatoes went down and now Golden Flake can make more money per bag of chips.
2. Available technology – Golden Flake just brought some new machines and can produce chips for less and make more money per bag.
3. Profitability of other goods – the price of corn went up and Golden Flake makes less money for every bag of corn chips it sells. Of course, Golden Flake wants to sell more potato chips, because they have a bigger profit margin.
4. The number of sellers in the market. Frito-Lay just went bankrupt and there are fewer people selling potato chips. Golden Flake would be happy to step in and sell more chips.

These factors are *supply shifters*. In short, many factors can affect supply and demand.

Elasticity

Now let's move on to another important economic concept. Elasticity.

Elasticity measures *how* sensitive we are to changes in price. Golden Flake raises the price of chips – will it sell more bags of chips or fewer bags of chips? If we really don't care how much we pay for a bag of Golden Flake chips and they bump up the price from $2 a bag to $2.25 a bag, we will still be willing to buy.

Of course there is the other reaction. "What, Golden Flake is 25 cents more a bag? Heck with that!"

If you really don't care that Golden Flake has increased its price by 25 cents or even 50 cents or even a dollar – you can say that the demand for Golden Flake chips is 'inelastic'. You and other consumers are willing to pay almost any price for that bag of chips.

But in the real world, you are not going to pay that much more for a bag of Golden Flake chips; you will just switch to another variety of chip. In reality, the demand for Golden Flake chips is 'elastic'. You and other Golden Flake fans will only pay a certain price or a narrow range of prices for Golden Flake chips.

The makers of Golden Flake chips know this and that is why, as we will discuss later, they know that they can only sell a bag of chips for $2 a bag. That means that when the government raises taxes or sewer fees or the cost of potatoes increases, Golden Flake has to find some way of absorbing that cost because it cannot pass it on to the consumer.

Determinants of elasticity

What determines elasticity? In other words, what determines if people will pay any price for a product, if the demand for that product is inelastic (a good way to remember this is to remember the word 'in' – like insatiable)? What determines if people will only pay so much for a product, if the demand is 'elastic' (think that the product price always snaps back to its original price)?

Well if there are close substitutes, it is hard to raise your price. That is why it is hard for Golden Flake to raise its prices; you will just buy another cheaper snack food. Plus there are so many chip competitors, people will just switch to another brand.

What if the price of gas went to over four dollars a gallon (right – like *that* would happen). Well, unless you have a Flintstone car and can pedal your way to work, there aren't any substitutes for gas and you will pay what the market demands. So the demand for gas is inelastic, you got to have it.

Equilibrium Price

If you have read any economics textbooks at all, you know they all preach that consumer behavior follows the law of supply and demand. It is common sense that the lower the price, the more product the consumer will demand. If Golden Flake lowers the price of potato chips from $2 a bag to $1 a bag, customers will buy more potato chips.

But if customers are more than happy to buy potato chips for $3 a bag, compared to $2 a bag, Golden Flake will be happy to stock the grocery shelves with bags of chips.

Which brings us to another economics term – 'equilibrium price' – which means that Golden Flake would set the price of chips as high as it could, heck who doesn't like excessive profit? Of course the only flaw in this great idea is that people would buy substitute goods.

Yep, that is another economics term we have touched upon earlier. Substitute goods. I remember my economics teacher going on and on about that term: substitute goods. And I could never figure out why; we ain't talking rocket science here. Substitute goods means that if Golden Flake prices their chips too high, you will buy corn chips or pretzels or some other snack food instead. You will substitute some other snack, some other salty cheaper food for potato chips. Another simple way of looking at 'substitute goods' is if steak is too high, you will buy hamburger.

I wonder if my ex-teacher is now retired sitting on the retirement house porch going on and on about substitute goods until his wife, after 50 years, goes berserk, slaps him upside the head and says, "Oh shut up, Henry. I should have found a substitute for you years ago."

The point is that Golden Flake can't price their chips too high; no one will buy them. Golden Flake can't price them too low, they have to make a profit. The 'equilibrium price' is the price the consumers will buy chips and be happy and Golden Flake can sell chips, make a decent profit and be happy.

Exceptions to the Rule

There are some exceptions to this rule though. Even in the world of chips.

Sometimes a good or service is demanded due to its rarity or 'snob' value. The more limited an item is, the higher its 'snob' value. Take the example of rare art pieces, or designer clothing or vintage cars whose values are so high just because they are rare. Some consumers will desire and buy the rarest form of goods at very expensive prices and this behavior is called the snob effect.

Golden Flake has used 'snob appeal' in the past. Whenever the University of Alabama won a national football championship, Golden Flake would issue a 'collector tin' which would feature highlights of the championship season. Limited tins were offered to Alabama football fans and Golden Flake was able to sell them at a much higher price than a regular bag of chips. After all, if a collector tin of chips is priced close to the price of a regular bag of chips, where is the perceived snob appeal?

The Veblen Effect

Now, I love this term and it is fun to toss around at parties. Of course it is tough to work into a conversation and when you do, people tend to drift away, but hey that's another story.

The term is the Veblen Effect. The Veblen effect occurs when the customer demands a good as long as its price is high. Think about expensive wine. If the price falls, the product loses its 'value' and hence its consumers move on to the next expensive item.

The Veblen effect is a great way of making a profit. Think about Ralph Lauren shirts. There is not a Ralph Lauren factory that just makes Ralph Lauren shirts. They are produced in factories around the world, the same factories that make every other polo shirt, including the ones you buy at Walmart for five bucks.

Not to get all political here, but any company wants to produce its product as cheaply as possible and sell it for as much as it can. Golden Flake is not going to look for ways to increase its production costs; rather it will continue to search for more cost-effective ways to make chips.

And many of your clothes are made in Third World countries that pay labor very little money. In fact, the National Labor Committee observed these working conditions firsthand while investigating 21 factories in China producing some of the most common clothing products sold in the US.

- 10 to 15 hour shifts per day
- 60 to 90 hour work weeks
- 6 and 7 workdays a week
- below subsistence wages of 13 to 28 cents an hour with no benefits
- forced, uncompensated overtime
- unsafe and unsanitary working environments
- housing in crowded dormitories

- 24 hour surveillance

The National Labor Committee's report specified the practices of several companies.

- Walmart was manufacturing Kathie Lee Gifford's line of handbags in the Liang Shi factory in China where factory workers labored 10 hours a day, six and seven days a week. Warehouse workers earned as little as $0.12 an hour.
- Ralph Lauren blouses, which sell for $88 in the US, were made by young women working these 12 to 15 hour shifts, 6 days a week at 23 cents an hour.
- Ann Taylor jackets and skirts selling for $200 each are made by workers under similar conditions, paid 14 cents an hour.
- $90 Liz Claiborne blouses were made by workers paid 25 cents an hour.
- $65 Limited men's shirts made by workers paid 32 cents an hour.
- JC Penny's clothes made at 18 cents an hour.
- Workers in Kmart factories made 28 cents an hour.

Okay – this is not a book on sweatshops, but it does show the power of the Veblen effect. You can take a polo shirt, made in the same sweatshop, and sell it at Walmart for five dollars or take the same shirt, stick a fancy logo on it and sell it for $50. Gotta love the Veblen effect.

The Real World of Golden Flake
Cost-benefit analysis of a new machine:

Any foreign substance in any bag of chips can turn into a major headache and an expensive proposition for any chip manufacturer.

So you want to check the bags before they go out and make

sure there is no broken metal in them, from the machines, no plastic – there should only be chips in that bag.

And technology is always advancing and we are always posing the age-old question for management – WHEN do you invest in technology?

An x-ray unit can run up to 150,000 bucks, and you used to have to buy one for each line. They used to be able to scan only items with the same density. For instance you can't send a corn chip through the same x-ray machine with the pork skins.

They have different densities – so you have to set up the lines so the pork skins and the puff items would go through one x-ray machine, because both of those items are close to each other in density. But a different x-ray machine needs to be set up for tortilla and corn chips.

But now they have x-ray machines that can do all items.

So when do you invest in x-ray machines? Do you keep waiting for better versions to come out?

It's a management question you deal with on a regular basis.

– *David Jones*

Supply and Demand don't mean a thing if you can't get your product in the store

This whole company depends on four feet of space in a store. It also depends on the geographic location of the store – in Alabama we will get more than four feet, outside of Alabama, where our sphere of influence decreases proportionate to the miles away from our Birmingham office – we get less space – but here in Alabama we can double, triple, even quadruple our space.

In the convenience stores, we will get 50% of the space, position sometimes, position meaning the first salty snack you see when the consumer comes into the store.

And so our market share here, our tradition, our history tells us that, because we can turn the product that allows us to generate enough revenue to maintain that kind of spacing allocation in Alabama.

When you go outside it is a little different – even though we are known we are not as well known.

But, you got to have space in the store to have sales. And it can be difficult to get space in any store; you have to have a proven record of product movement. The stores don't have time to take up space with items that do not turn.

In short, gaining space in stores is really a derivative of the sales that you have. If you can go to the store manager and say, "Look, Joe, I have x number of foot of space and I am selling out before I can get back to your store. My route does not allow me to get back sooner; therefore I need an extra foot or two of space."

On an individual basis it is easy to do that if you revert back to those five points of selling, if you have built that good will, then Joe will allow you to have that space.

However, if you are talking to a major corporation and they have 50 to 100 stores and you are talking to that buyer in that home office that makes that decision for all 100 of those stores at the same time, that is a bit of a different story. However, you can still put together a reference to the amount of volume that is turned per linear foot of space that you have in the store and if that exceeds what this buyer's goal is, then you have a legitimate shot at asking for additional space.

In the real world, you often get into a situation where you have to pay for that space; I am not talking paying the person, but legally and upfront pay the store chain a rebate or pay them dollars per foot of shelf space to buy that space for a 12-month period. That goes on day in and day out everywhere you go, when you are the manufacturer/distributor.

But before you pay for space, you have to do an analysis to

see if the payments they want justify the money invested. You have to turn enough product to offset the increased cost of business.

In fact we are going to go visit a chain of stores tomorrow and that very thing is going to be part of the topic. I will personally be bringing up to the chain store the money we are spending today with them in order to rent the space relative to the revenue we are generating out the front door.

Hmm and it is a little bit out of kilter, so I have to make the decision: Do I want to keep that business or can I negotiate my agreement with them down or how can I figure out how to sell more product to justify paying for the space. Selling more products to pay for the space is the best way. That reduces my percent of the cost of doing business. Yet, therein lays the rub, figuring out a way to generate enough revenue so renting the store space is being a profitable venture for everyone involved.

In short, sales often is a moving target, there are no hard and fast rules. You can try and apply them sometimes, but you have to take each individual situation on its value and make a decision the best you can at the time.

I will say this, there are more and more major chains electing not to participate in space payments or rebates payments, and they are flat electing to let sales per foot dictate the amount of space you have, so we like that.
– *Randy Bates*

Forget supply and demand – your competitors drive the price

We are very sensitive to price and we are in the position that many other categories are in the store: if the leader does not move, it is difficult for the regionals to move. So unfortunately we have to follow the leader.

If Frito-Lay does not increase prices, we can't either. And it doesn't matter how it is impacting our bottom line. But we also know they can't make a bag of potato chips any cheaper than we can, but we have to follow Frito-Lay's prices.

In short, all regional players follow the leader and if the leader is making moves, then we are allowed to make moves too. But Golden Flake can't go out and be higher than Frito-Lay is on a per ounce basis at a retail level. You can be lower, you can be equal, but if you try to be higher, that is a formula for disaster.

Because you cannot raise prices, you always are adjusting. If gas prices go up, you have to make changes in your everyday expenses, we reroute routes to reduce mileage, we reduce promotional expenditures, and for instance we are significantly under our level for promotional spending today as compared to three years ago due to high gas prices. We had to adjust.

We knew these things were coming – you have to be able to look ahead and not get surprised. So we begin a phased-in program aimed at reducing our promotional activities to the point of where we are selling more of our products at face value today than in my 30 years.

Face value is the pre-price that is on the bag as opposed to a promoted reduced price for the consumer. And then ultimately in those expense reductions, you have to cut back on marketing too.

We have done a real good job of reducing our production activities, so much so that I can put on pressure to increase our marketing budgets. Because you have to spend money one way or the other, you have to spend money to push it out the front door or to bring them in the front door, one or the other.

If you don't do either one, there will come a point in time when you will die on the vine. Because your competitor will do one or both. Push the product out the front door and bring customers in.

You either go through a period of time when you are just dealing it, reducing the retail price to entice the consumer to buy it when they get in the door and that is okay if you can balance it and not deal everything. Preferably, what we ask our marketing people to do is run a marketing program that makes consumers want to go in front door looking for Golden Flake.

And that is the preferable way, you get to expose your brand to a multitude and it gets a much better chance of getting people to come into the store looking for Golden Flake as opposed to only targeting people who are in the store.

We are fighting the 500-pound gorilla out there, Frito-Lay, who can spend money on both ends of the spectrum all they want to. We are fortunate to be in a spot today where we can spend more on marketing and spend less on promotional activities.

– Randy Bates

Costs and benefits: corn chips vs. potato chips

Why are corn chips are more profitable than potato chips?

On potato chips, when you buy 100 pounds of potatoes you only get to sell 20 pounds. Because the potato is 75% water and when you are cooking it you lose all of that weight, but in the mornings when our cookers are going if you are on the freeway you can look over and see the smoke coming out of here – well that is not smoke, that is steam and that is profit going up the stack. We have to pay a full price for the 100 pounds of potato, but we can only sell 25 pounds of them.

Conversely, on all corn-based products, every 100 pounds of corn, you get to sell 110 pounds because you don't lose anything in the process of mashing the corn and turning it into a flat tortilla and then adding salt and adding seasoning. So you can see that corn-based products are more profitable than potato products, although potato products represent about 45% of our business.

We always like to sell a bunch of corn-based products even though potato has the lion share of the business; we still make a little money on potato products, but you always try to expand your business based on corn products.

The difference between corn and potato products, the bottom line varies about three points; on a bag of potato chips, when it is all said and done, in today's world, with raw material costs the way they are and the selling and delivery and gas prices, for every dollar, we put about a penny in the bank.

And on tortillas and corn-based products we put three to four cents in the bank when everything works the way it is supposed to. I am talking averages, right now it is worse than that – potato costs, cooking oil, natural gas, corn prices – it is horrendous right now – you have to make up for it in distribution.

– *Mark McCutcheon*

Selling that bag for 99 cents or More costs and benefits

At the end of the day we have to sell you a bag of chips for 99 cents. That makes us ask how many bags of chips at 99 cents are we going have to sell to cover this – the cost of health care, the cost of the sewer bill, the cost of raw materials, the cost of gas.

And when someone comes to me and needs a new machine or a new truck or anything, they also have to explain to me how they are going to get this money back. How is it going to impact the bottom line?

And we know that 99 cent bag of chips is our revenue and it has to pay for everything this company does. That is why we keep looking at alternative solutions, at better ways of doing things.

We don't understand the large company or the big group that gets a bailout from the government, and then they go on this big outing.
— *Mark McCutcheon*

Choosing what to sell: costs and benefits

We placed some products that we did not go forward with; one for example was a kettle-fired potato chip. They were outstanding. They were terrific; the problem was they were labor intensive to produce and there simply was not enough demand for the product in the market. You could not create the critical mass that you needed to make it go.

You only have so much space in the store, and it used to be that you had to pay for every single inch of space in a store. That started back in the snack wars. But anyway, if you don't get the volume and the movement, you can't take space for a product that sells three a week to something that sells 30 a week.

We also made a baked potato chip. We still sell it but we let someone else make it and the reason was that it wasn't good; it was terrific. But we did not have the volume. People talk about healthier food, but the fact is people want a good tasting potato chip; they want a good tasting snack. You don't go on a diet and eat snacks that are not the idea of a diet.

So we decided that we are going to emphasize outstanding snacks, they are what they are. People eat them because they like them, it makes them feel good and we are going to make that kind of product.
— *Wayne Pate*

Stocking Fees and the Snack Wars: Forget supply and demand

There was a time, and I remember that these were wonderful days, that we did our business based on a few simple things.

Having good relationships with the stores, which we were able to do as well or better than anybody. Having great products which we could do, and being a dependable supplier. You were able to do business because you satisfied people. And they knew who you were and you worked with them. Those were the days when you earned the business, because you helped the customer.

And then comes along a company called Eagle Snacks. Eagle was a company started by Anheuser-Busch. They decided they would be in the snack business. We already go to the stores so we are going to get in the snack business and it will be a fit to sell snacks with our other products.

They didn't understand the market, but they had a ton of money behind their new snack food company... So in order to gain space – because before this, no one was paying for space. We got the space because we earned it. We earned it because we sold product and serviced it well and that service and our relationships got us the space. We would go help the stores. We gained space because we went in there and worked with them.

So when Eagle comes in, we have space and someone else has space and there is no space for Eagle. So Eagle starts proposing to the stores, "We are going to pay you for the space. You give us four feet or six feet or eight feet and we will give you so many dollars per foot."

The store begins to go, "Hey, they are giving me money up front. I believe I will take it."

And that moves us down or Frito-Lay down or somebody down or they expand the section. Most of the time they did not expand the section, except they took the space from someone else and gave it to Eagle Snacks.

Well Frito-Lay said, "They are not going to take one dime of business from us and they are never going to make a profit, trying to compete against us."

Well, we had been doubling in size every five years for 40 years until the mid-eighties. And we said, "Okay we have two elephants fighting. They have more money than we have. We can't get in a money war with them because we will lose."

They both can outspend us. We know that. When it comes down to shelling out the money, the guy with the most snowballs will win the snowball fight.

But we said that we are going to keep doing the things we do well, but we are going to have to adopt tactics that will help us stay in business, because one day a lot of people won't be around anymore. But we will be here, Frito-Lay will be here. We're not sure who else will be here, but Golden Flake will still be here.

So we started operating on the basis that we are going to survive all of this. Frito-Lay started buying space and stores, some customers that in the beginning couldn't buy anything, who couldn't pay us, who we had helped during tough times and who we had helped grow from nothing into something, these very stores we had given credit and who we had helped grow came to us and said, "You are going to have to pay us."

We said. "We are?" "You can't remember when?"

So people started walking in with their checkbooks and started paying for space. So we had to start paying for space. Well that cuts down on the profit pretty quick. And then the space we are allocated is not based on what the consumer will buy or how good of a reputation you got, it's based on who gave you the most money for it.

That doesn't seem to be a good way to run a business. But that is the way it happened. So we got hurt and some companies went out of business. That went on for 17 years. And Eagle Snack never made a penny of profit. Finally, one day, someone apparently says to August Busch, "How much longer are you going to keep throwing money away on this Eagle Snack business?"

He shut it down. They sold four plants to Frito-Lay and we bought a couple of their trucks. In record speed they shut that thing down. We thought Frito-Lay would take a little different approach when that happened. But Frito-Lay had gotten used to paying for space and they decided that they would keep fighting to put everybody out of business.

And they still are.

We are a big subject with Frito-Lay. We have had people tell us that they get up every day thinking how they can hurt Golden Flake because we are one of the regional companies they have a hard time dealing with.

They have hurt our profits during the years, but we are still here and trying to do it right.

And I am not just talking about their ambitions. We have had people come and tell us how they try to attack us and hurt us. They have hurt us, there's no question about it.

We will keep doing our thing. We are going to keep making good stuff. We are going to service it well and hopefully the consumer will buy it.

Go downtown right now and I bet Frito-Lay is pushing Buy One, Get One for Free potato chips... And potatoes are at a record high, they have never cost this much... I guarantee that Frito-Lay is losing money on that promotion. It doesn't matter, they can hurt us.

What happened, through the years, Walmart came along and they wanted an everyday low price. They didn't want money up front. They wanted money every day, so we had to agree with Walmart that they gave us the space, but we had to give them a price so they could sell at their everyday low price.

Several more companies have decided now that they are not going to make you pay for space. What was happening, they started making money off the purchasing of space and not making any money on the retail end of the business. Well they are supposed to be making money doing retail groceries. And that interferes with the consumer wanting to buy something. You are offering him what you want now, based on what somebody paid to put it there.

They will give you a song and dance about how they decided to stock their shelves, but the fact is they made their decision based who gave them the most money for the space.

That has subsided some, and we have gotten away from that to a large degree and we try to say, "Look, let's assign space on what we can do on a volume, instead of money up front, and let's try to meet an everyday low price."

Not every store today you have to buy space from. Some still want some upfront money. But it all started with Eagle Snack Foods back in the mid-eighties.

— *Wayne Pate*

Chapter 15

Multiplier Effect

Introduction: We have taken quite a journey. Now we reach a very important economic principle. The Multiplier Effect. Simply put, a lawyer produces nothing that can be sold and resold and that can create jobs. Making a product does create a variety of jobs. Let's explore the Multiplier Effect.

> Quote: Being busy does not always mean real work. The object of all work is production or accomplishment and to either of these ends there must be foresight, system, planning, intelligence and honest purpose, as well as perspiration. Seeming to do is nothing.
>
> *– Thomas Edison*

Why is it important to produce something, to make something? Even a bag of chips or a soft drink? The Multiplier Effect is a crucial term for anyone to understand if they want to help the economy grow and create jobs.

Recently, the President was on TV bragging about his new economic stimulus program and noted that Columbus, Ohio, because of government help, had hired seven more policemen. This could be the worst possible use of stimulus money.

Policemen do not create or build anything. Sure they might take their salary and take their uniforms to the dry cleaner and buy more groceries and maybe even buy a new car and that might help the economy.

But if you had given that money to a Widget factory, they could have hired more workers to build more widgets. Why is that a more valuable use of money?

Welcome to the world of the Multiplier Effect. Let's take a

closer look.

If you hire a cop, you do not create other jobs. You merely have placed another civic servant on the tax rolls that business must pay for. And if business pays more taxes, that is less money they have to hire workers.

You can argue we need more cops to stop crime. But if we create jobs to hire people, that also will be effective in stopping crime. People with full-time jobs rarely commit crimes.

Remember the concept of limited resources; Golden Flake has only so much money to spend. And when it sends money to the government in the form of taxes to pay for that new cop, it cannot hire a worker or buy a new machine or expand its market.

If you create a job in manufacturing, you create other jobs. Simple – yes. Companies making a product create other jobs such as natural gas, phone services, and packing materials. In addition, workers use their pay to buy goods and services from other companies and these companies also hire employees. These downstream employment impacts from a particular industry are called the multiplier effect.

Here are the industries that Golden Flake impacts when it makes a potato chip:

Direct
Food Processing
Wholesale Trade
Business Services
Retail Trade
Real Estate
Pulp & Paper
Motor Freight & Transport
Printing & Publishing
Banking
Health Services
Communications

Professional Services
Construction
Utilities
Chemicals & Allied Products
Fabricated Metal
Automotive Services
Insurance Carriers
Hotels & Lodging Places
Security & Commodity Brokers
Legal Services
State & Local Non-Education Government
Credit Agencies
Railroads & Related Services
Recreation Services
Petroleum Products
Non-Profit Organizations
Social Services
Education Services
Stone, Glass & Clay
Repair Services
Motion Pictures
Air Transportation
Personal Services
Transportation Equipment
Federal Non-Military
Transportation Services
Industrial Machinery
Electrical Equipment
Insurance Agents & Brokers
Water Transportation
Apparel
Miscellaneous Manufacturing
Local, Interurban Passenger Transit
Furniture

Agricultural Services
Scientific Instruments
Primary Metals
Wood Products
Domestic Services
Farms
Rubber Products
Leather Products
Oil Mining
Pipe Lines, Except Natural Gas

Make SOMETHING

In other words, producing SOMETHING is good business as it spreads wealth throughout the economy.

If you produce something, even a potato, you are affecting numerous other areas of our economy.

Think about that. Again, if the government hires another employee, that employee is not producing anything. He is not adding jobs to the economy. But, we all must pay for his salary, office space and benefits. Paying for that salary takes money away from me. That means I can't go out to dinner as often to help the new restaurant down the street, I may wash my own clothes instead of having them dry-cleaned, I will make my own coffee at home, instead of buying coffee at Starbucks and I might buy one bag of Golden Flake chips instead of two bags of Golden Flake chips.

Again, Golden Flake also pays for that new government employee through their taxes. That means they can't hire an employee, introduce a new product, and pay dividends.

The worst part is that the new government employee does not have a multiplier effect. He makes no products, so he doesn't have to buy any raw materials. He has no factory, so he doesn't have to pay a mortgage, buy new equipment, pay employees a salary, pay the light and water bills, and doesn't have to hire salesmen to sell his product or truck drivers to deliver it.

Lessons on production from our hero: The Potato

How important is producing something?

Let's look at the simple potato, after all this is *Potato Chip Economics*.

Let's look at just one state – Texas. What kinds of jobs does producing, growing the simple potato create?

So what? What effect could that have upon the economy?

Total employment associated with the South Texas potato industry is estimated to be 2,679 jobs. Farm employment represents 656 of those jobs. The balance of employment, 2,023 jobs, is located in non-farm sectors of the Texas economy.

The sectors include: food and beverages, 691 jobs; truck transportation, 213 jobs; wholesale trade, 141 jobs; and agriculture support services such as sorting, grading, cleaning and packing, 80 jobs.

But wait, producing that simple Texas potato has indirect effects. How about the industries supplying goods and services required to produce and market potatoes. These include: agriculture support activities, $2.5 million; wholesale trade, $25.3 million; real estate, $8.0 million; truck transportation, $23.9 million; pesticide manufacturing, $1.5 million; and farm machinery, $184,000. Food and beverage sales at $40.3 million, insurance and banking services at $6.0 million, and health care at $5.3 million are supported by household incomes.

That is just by growing a potato. And how many jobs does hiring a new government worker produce?

The Real World of Golden Flake

One hundred jobs at Golden Flake support at least 195 jobs outside of Golden Flake. Think about the farmer who provides the potatoes, the trucker who delivers the shipment, and the retailer who sells the final product.

That two dollars that you spend on a bag of Golden Flake chips really ends up being distributed through a complex chain of suppliers and distributors and eventually filters down to the farmer to help him meet the many expenses in running a farm and even maintaining his tractor.

Although we only see that bag of chips on the grocery shelf, the entire system that Golden Flake is part of sprawls clear across the country and employs millions of people.

According the US Department or Agriculture, you got to love the numbers they keep track of; there are over 2 million farms across the United States. Production from these farms is purchased and processed by over 25,000 food and beverage companies. These companies, in turn, sell their production to nearly 33,000 food wholesalers, 113,000 food retailers, and 378,000 foodservice companies. The food products are then sold and distributed to over 111 million households throughout the US. About 25 million people are employed in the food marketing.

The point of all those numbers, besides giving the USDA a chance to show off, shows how extensive the food network is that Golden Flake is part of.

Another fun fact. When you spend a dollar on a bag of Golden Flake chips, where did that dollar go to?

Thirty-nine cents goes to off-farm labor, 8 cents goes to packaging, 4 cents goes to transportation, 4 cents goes to energy, 5 cents goes to profit, 4 cents goes to advertising, 4 cents goes to depreciation, 4 cents go to rent, 3 cents goes to paying interest, 2 cents goes to repairs, 4 cents goes to business taxes and 19 cents goes to the farmer.

Food production, and again making a bag of chips is part of that process, is BIG business. Consider these numbers. The food business spends over 275 billion dollars a year on labor, over 57 billion on packaging, over 29 billion on transportation, over 25 billion on fuel and electricity, over 33 billion on pretax corporate profits, over 29 billion on advertising, over 20 billion on interest, over 31 billion on rent and over 25 billion on business taxes.

Lesson Five

Balance Sheets, Income Statements,

Cash Flow – Oh My!

Introduction: To really understand a company you must be able to analyze its performance from a financial standpoint. All public companies are required to file quarterly and annual financial statements, and these statements are rife with information about a company's health and profitability. It is important to be financially literate, and this means having a working knowledge of the three main financial statements – the balance sheet, the income statement, and the statement of cash flows. The fourth financial statement is the statement of owner's equity, but for our purposes we will focus on the three statements mentioned above.

The sheer volume of information found in an annual report can be overwhelming, but the basics outlined in the following chapters will enable you to analyze a company's financial condition without getting lost in the weeds. As we walk through Golden Flake's balance sheet, income statement, and statement of cash flows, you will see that much of finance and accounting is easy to grasp, and oftentimes intuitive. Keep in mind that if any questions arise while reviewing a company's financial statements, you can always look to 'management's discussion and analysis', or MD&A, to see if there is any clarification. These next few chapters won't make you an expert by any means, but knowing these basics will give you the confidence to look at a set of financial statements and make sense of them.

Chapter 16

The Balance Sheet Explained

One of my good friends was interviewing for a position in capital planning at a large multinational bank. Right out of the gate, the first question posed to him was, which financial statement do you think is the most important? Now, most non-business people would immediately say the income statement – it is after all called the 'profit and loss statement', and why do companies exist if not to make a profit? But the truth is that it doesn't matter how large your bottom line is if you don't have a strong balance sheet. Assets and liabilities may not be as sensational as earnings, but they give vital information about the health of a company.

My friend, having completed his MBA just a year before, was wise to the question and answered balance sheet (in post-interview discussion, it was revealed that the statement of cash flows was also an acceptable answer, but more on that later). He understood that the balance sheet is an essential accounting tool – it tells us how a company is funded, what it has and what it owes, and its ultimate net worth.

The first thing to know about a balance sheet is that it represents a specific point in time. Unlike an income statement, which shows a company's operations over a period of time, like a fiscal quarter or a year, the balance sheet is a snapshot. On most balance sheets, as demonstrated with Golden Flake, there will be 'As of' at the top of the page, followed by a date. For example this particular balance sheet tells us that as of 11/28/2008 Golden Flake had $4.62 million in inventory, the same way that on 11/28/2008 I had a car, an apartment, and some lingering student loan debt.

Taking a high-level view of the balance sheet is helpful in understanding why it is so important. A balance sheet tells us what a company owns, and what it owes. The difference between what it owns and what it owes is equity, or the value of ownership interest.

The balance sheet contains information about two vital things – a company's **liquidity**, and its **leverage**. These are two words that people like to say with a lot of pomp and circumstance, but are really quite easy to understand. Liquidity simply means a company's ability to pay its short-term debts. This is important, as a company doesn't have very much longevity if they can't meet their current obligations. Leverage, on the other hand, is the extent to which a company uses debt to support its total assets. If a company is relying too much on debt to fund its operations, this could be a red flag. Tied to the idea of leverage is a company's **capital structure** – another term that analysts love to use but is very easy to understand. A company's capital structure is the proportion of debt and equity. You want your company to have a suitable capital structure and appropriate leverage, so it can be successful in the long-term.

The Basics

Before we dive into Golden Flake's financials, it's important to know the basic components of any balance sheet. The balance sheet is broken into three key sections – **Assets, Liabilities and Shareholders' Equity**.

Assets – assets are what a company uses to operate its business. Common asset categories include inventory, cash, and property, plant and equipment (PP&E). For example Golden Flake uses their assets, potatoes and machines, to operate their business and make potato chips. Think of assets as resources that a company has to produce their product or service.

Liabilities – in the simplest form, liabilities are what a company owes. Common liabilities include short and long-term borrowings, and any money that is owed to suppliers, owners, or others.

Shareholders' Equity – this is perhaps the most abstract component of the balance sheet. Shareholder's equity typically comes from two main sources – money that was invested in the company, and retained earnings. Retained earnings are accumulated profits that a business has held on to, and not given out to shareholders in the form of dividends. Shareholders' equity represents a company's net worth; it is what is available to shareholders after all creditors and debts have been paid off.

A Balancing Act

The balance sheet, as the name cleverly suggests, must balance. Logically this makes sense, as a company must pay for what it has (assets) by either borrowing funds (liabilities), or receiving funds from shareholders (shareholders' equity). This balance is represented in the equation:

Assets = Liabilities + Shareholders' Equity

Think about what this equation means – basically, the total assets of a business must be supported by an equal amount of claims against those assets. The claims of the creditors are liabilities, while the claims of the owners are shareholders' equity. A good way to remember this equation is 'ALE' (Asset = Liabilities + Equity), or the beverage you probably want to drink after looking at a balance sheet.

The Real Deal

Now, let's take a quick walk through Golden Flake's balance sheet. This statement starts, as almost all balance sheets do, with current assets.

Assets

Current Assets – One of the perks of working in finance or business is that if you don't know the meaning of a term, most of the time you can just rearrange the words and present a definition. For example, current assets are the assets on your balance sheet that are current. Essentially, these are assets that can be reasonably expected to convert to cash over the next 12 months.

Current assets are listed in descending order of their expected conversion to cash. Cash, for obvious reasons, is listed first, followed by short-term investments. Although Golden Flake did not have any short-term investments at 11/28/2008, this category represents funds placed in securities, typically stocks or bonds that will expire within 12 months.

Accounts Receivable – You can see that as of 11/28/2008, Golden Flake had $7.96 million in Accounts Receivable, Net. In many cases when a company makes a sale, they extend credit rather than immediately collecting money from customers. So this category represents funds owed to the company. A net figure is the figure that remains when everything that should be subtracted has already been subtracted (like net income). In this case, net accounts receivable means the allowance for doubtful accounts has already been subtracted. Allowance for doubtful accounts is just what it sounds like – these are accounts that you just don't think will ever be paid back.

Inventory – Inventory is what a company has that will be ready, or is already ready, for sale. Inventory can be further broken into raw materials, work in process, or finished goods. Golden Flake had $4.62 million in inventory at 11/28/2008, which can be further broken into raw materials (potatoes), work in process (half-formed bags of potato chips), and finished goods (bags of chips that are ready to go to you and me).

Inventory Turnover – For manufacturing companies especially, it is important to monitor inventory. Inventory turnover – how quickly you can sell and replace your inventory – lets you know how efficient a company is at converting their inventory into sales. This is calculated by dividing Cost of Goods Sold (taken from the income statement, and explained in that chapter) by average inventory, or:

Cost of Goods Sold / Average Inventory

A high inventory turnover figure generally means better performance, while a low figure could mean that a company is holding on to their inventory for too long, which could lead to overstocking and the risk of obsolescence. However, there are exceptions to this rule, and it is important to compare a company's inventory turnover ratio to other companies in the same industry to get a good idea of what is normal.

Prepaid Expenses – As of 11/28/2008, Golden Flake had $2.0 million in prepaid expenses. This category represents payments the business has made for goods or services yet to be received. These are current assets, because the company has the right to receive the product in the near future. Typical examples include prepaid insurance or prepaid rent.

Non-current Assets – Following current assets on the balance sheet are non-current assets, or assets that are not expected to be converted into cash within the next year. From a lending perspective, non-current assets are vital as they are the source of repayment for long-term loans.

Fixed Assets or Property, Plant and Equipment (PP&E) – These are the physical assets used to produce goods and services; typical fixed asset categories include land, buildings, equipment, and machinery. Fixed assets have a much longer useful life than current assets, and these are typically non-trading assets – they are not sold directly to a company's customers. But fixed assets will not last forever, and the value of the asset will decrease over its life. Therefore important to the concept of fixed assets is **depreciation**, or the process of allocating the cost of an asset over its useful life.

Intangibles – Intangibles are just what they sound like, they are assets that cannot be seen or touched and may not be realizable in the form of cash. Examples of intangible assets include patents, copyrights, trademarks, goodwill, or other items that are not physical in nature.

On Golden Flake's balance sheet you can see that current assets + non-current assets = total assets. This holds true for all balance sheets, and following the same logic, current liabilities + non-current liabilities = total liabilities.

Liabilities

As discussed above, liabilities are any obligations that are due to be paid.

Current Liabilities – As with assets, current liabilities are listed first, as they are obligations that are expected to be settled in cash within the next 12 months.

Accounts Payable – As of 11/28/2008, you can see that Golden Flake recorded $3.83 million in accounts payable. While accounts receivable represent funds that are owed to a company, accounts payable represents funds that a company owes to its suppliers. Companies will often make purchases using credit, and accounts payable is the amount of money that a company owes to its vendors.

Accrued Expenses – Accrued expenses are the opposite of prepaid expenses. With prepaid expenses, you have paid for something but not yet received the good or service. With accrued expenses, the expense is recognized before cash is paid out. A typical example is accrued salaries and benefits – wages can be accrued for an entire week or a two-week period before they are paid out (and hence why paycheck Friday is such a joyous affair).

Notes Payable/Short-Term Debt – You can see that as of 11/28/2008, Golden Flake had $2.0 million in notes payable or short-term debt. A note payable is a written promise, or note, to repay a specific amount (usually with interest) on a specific date. Notes payable are useful in helping a company meet their short-term funding needs.

Current Portion of Long-Term Debt (CPLTD) – CPLTD is the amount of long-term debt that must be paid off in the next 12 months. Companies will typically enter into credit facilities with multi-year terms, for example three or five years. However, depending on the terms with the bank, certain portions of this debt will come due each year, and must be paid back – hence we have CPLTD. However, if you do not have long-term debt (as Golden Flake does not) you will not have a CPLTD unless your credit facility is maturing that year.

Non-current Liabilities – Current liabilities are followed by non-current liabilities, or long-term financial obligations with a term greater than one year.

Long-Term Debt – One of the most important non-current liabilities is long-term debt. This is usually the first place I look in the liability section to get an idea of a company's financing and structure. Long-term debt can include bank loans, company bond issues, long-term leases, or any other financing agreement with a term greater than one year. It is important to get a breakdown of a company's long-term debt to understand what they owe, as these obligations are often several years in tenure and can limit a company's flexibility in the long-term. As you can see, at 11/28/2008, Golden Flake did not record any long-term debt, which indicates that their total debt is comprised of their notes payable, and due within the next year.

Shareholders' Equity

Shareholders' Equity is the portion of the company that is owned by the shareholders. This equity is generated through original investment in the company, purchase of ownership directly from the company, or through retained earnings. On Golden Flake's balance sheet the largest equity categories are common stock, additional paid-in capital, retained earnings, and treasury stock. This balance sheet is very typical, and demonstrates the structure that you will encounter on most balance sheets.

Common Stock – Many people can be confused by the idea of common stock, but the concept is really quite straightforward. Common stock represents a piece of ownership. When I buy stock in a company, I am essentially purchasing a piece of that company. My ownership percentage will depend on how many shares I have, and how many shares there are total. Holders of common stock usually have voting rights, meaning they can exercise some form of control, but in the event of bankruptcy common stockholders are repaid after all debtors and preferred stockholders are paid. Although Golden Flake did not have any preferred stock on their balance sheet, it's good to know what this is as well. Preferred shares also represent ownership in a company, but preferred stockholders typically do not have voting rights. Preferred stock is higher ranking than common stock, meaning preferred shareholders will be repaid ahead of common stockholders in the event of liquidation, and preferred stock usually has a priority over common stock in terms of dividends.

Additional Paid-In Capital – Additional paid-in capital is not typically a large component of a company's equity section, but it is useful to understand what this category represents. A par value is a stated value or face value – if a company issues stock with a certain par value, investors will sometimes pay more than this par value, or pay a premium. The excess paid by the investor over the par value is recorded in additional paid-in capital.

Treasury Stock – Treasury stock is easy to remember, because these are shares of stock that are kept in a company's treasury. These are shares that were either repurchased by the company, or never issued to the public in the first place.

Retained Earnings – We touched on retained earnings earlier, but it's important to understand what exactly this category means. If I have had a good year, then I will hopefully have positive net earnings. What I do with these net earnings will determine what happens to retained earnings. I essentially have two options – I can either issue a dividend, a payment to my shareholders, or I can reinvest this in my company. If I do **not** issue a dividend, then I am not paying anything out to my shareholders, and all of my net earnings will be reinvested in the company. If I **do** choose to issue a dividend, then I will take net earnings, subtract the dividend that made my shareholders happy, and reinvest the amount leftover in the company.

Using the Balance Sheet

That takes us through the three main categories of the balance sheet, and you can see that assets = liabilities + shareholder's equity. Now, let's go back to the ideas of liquidity and leverage discussed above. Balance sheets are great, but only if you use them to examine the health of the company.

Liquidity – the classic definition of liquidity is the ability to generate cash in order to make the payments on current liabilities. In essence, we assume that current liabilities will be paid from the conversion of current assets to cash. You certainly want a company to be able to pay their debts when and as they fall due.

Quick and Dirty Ratios: There are two ratios that are used as common measures of liquidity: the current ratio, and the quick ratio. By using these (very) simple ratios, you can get an understanding of how liquid a company really is.

The Current Ratio – as the name suggests, this is:

Current Assets / Current Liabilities

A ratio of 1:1 means that current assets could generate enough cash to cover current liabilities, and a high or rising current ratio indicates improving liquidity. Golden Flake demonstrates a favorable current ratio of 17.66 / 10.95, or 1.6.

The Quick Ratio – defined as:

Cash + Marketable Securities + Net Accounts Receivable / Current Liabilities

This is a stricter measure of liquidity, as it omits inventory as a way to pay for current liabilities, and will usually be lower than the current ratio. This holds true for Golden Flake, which shows a quick ratio of .95.

Leverage – As discussed earlier, leverage is the extent to which a company uses debt to support its assets. You don't want a company relying too much on debt, as this can severely limit management's operating flexibility. Common ways to measure leverage include:

The Debt to Asset Ratio: Total Liabilities / Total Assets
Or
The Debt to Equity Ratio: Total Liabilities / Shareholders' Equity

The debt to asset ratio indicates the proportion of assets that are financed by outside creditors. The debt to equity ratio, probably the most common leverage ratio, reveals how much capital was contributed by creditors, and how much by shareholders. It indicates how many dollars of outside financing there are for each dollar of owner's investment.

A certain amount of debt is acceptable, and indeed beneficial given tax related considerations; however, holding too much debt can present several problems. If a company is relying too heavily on debt to fund assets and operations, the debt can limit a company's flexibility, place pressure on the company to pay interest and principal, and equity will provide little cushion if asset values shrink. An acceptable debt to equity ratio will depend on a company's profitability, liquidity, stability, and the industry that it operates in.

Conclusion

It's important to compare a company's current balance sheet against past statements to identify any trends. If a company is increasing debt dramatically, depleting cash, building up inventory, or demonstrating other noticeable trends, you need to dig deeper to find the root cause. It's very easy to get lost when looking at a balance sheet – there are lots of marginal accounts, so you generally want to concern yourself with the *drivers* of the balance sheet. These are the largest accounts and will give you an indication of what is impacting the company – inventory, PP&E, intangibles, etc. A balance sheet reveals a great deal about a company, and with a basic understanding of assets, liabilities, and equity, you can understand what is driving a company's performance.

	As of	As of	As of	As of	As of
	2008-11-28	2008-08-29	2008-05-30	2008-02-29	2007-11-30
Cash & Equivalents	2.44	0.32	0.44	0.23	0.66
Short Term Investments	–	–	–	–	–
Cash and Short-Term Investments	2.44	0.32	0.44	0.23	0.66
Accounts Receivable – Trade, Net	7.96	8.01	7.94	7.39	7.65
Receivables – Other	–	–	–	–	–
Total Receivables, Net	7.96	8.01	7.94	7.45	7.71
Total Inventory	4.62	4.83	4.34	4.34	4.76
Prepaid Expenses	2.00	2.18	1.64	2.14	1.77
Other Current Assets, Total	0.65	0.65	0.65	0.58	0.58
Total Current Assets	**17.66**	**15.99**	**15.01**	**14.75**	**15.48**
Property/Plant/Equipment, Total – Gross	–	–	–	–	–
Goodwill, Net	–	–	–	–	–
Intangibles, Net	–	–	–	–	–
Long-Term Investments	–	–	–	–	–
Other Long-Term Assets, Total	2.29	2.46	2.59	2.93	2.86
Total Assets	**32.24**	**32.76**	**32.23**	**32.26**	**32.74**

Accounts Payable	3.83	4.66	3.57	2.66	3.45
Accrued Expenses	4.99	4.99	5.15	4.67	4.75
Notes Payable/Short-Term Debt	2.00	1.95	2.30	3.29	2.43
Current Port. of LT Debt/Capital Leases	–	–	0.00	0.00	0.00
Other Current Liabilities, Total	0.14	0.14	0.13	0.13	0.13
Total Current Liabilities	**10.95**	**11.73**	**11.15**	**10.74**	**10.75**
Long-Term Debt	–	–	–	–	–
Capital Lease Obligations	–	–	–	–	–
Total Long-Term Debt	**0.00**	**0.00**	**0.00**	**0.00**	**0.00**
Total Debt	**2.00**	**1.95**	**2.30**	**3.29**	**2.43**
Deferred Income Tax	0.62	0.62	0.62	0.75	0.75
Minority Interest	–	–	–	–	–
Other Liabilities, Total	1.46	1.48	1.50	1.52	1.54
Total Liabilities	**13.03**	**13.84**	**13.27**	**13.02**	**13.04**
Redeemable Preferred Stock, Total	–	–	–	–	–
Preferred Stock – Non Redeemable, Net	–	–	–	–	–
Common Stock, Total	9.22	9.22	9.22	9.22	9.22
Additional Paid-In Capital	6.50	6.50	6.50	6.50	6.50
Retained Earnings (Accumulated Deficit)	14.38	14.05	14.06	14.31	14.71
Treasury Stock – Common	-10.89	-10.84	-10.81	-10.79	-10.73
Other Equity, Total	–	–	–	–	–
Total Equity	**19.20**	**18.93**	**18.96**	**19.25**	**19.70**
Total Liabilities & Shareholders' Equity	**32.23**	**32.76**	**32.23**	**32.26**	**32.74**
Shares Outs – Common Stock					
Primary Issue	–	–	–	–	–
Total Common Shares	**11.75**	**11.78**	**11.79**	**11.79**	**11.82**

Chapter 17

The Income Statement

Overview

Despite the question posed to my friend in his interview, and his subsequent answer, the income statement is still vital to understanding a company's performance. The point the interviewer was trying to make is that people tend to focus exclusively on the income statement, when really the three financial statements need to be read in tandem. But there is a reason why the income statement is one of the major statements – it shows us whether or not a company is able to operate profitably.

Also called the profit and loss statement, earnings statement, or statement of operations, the income statement reveals whether a company made or lost money during a specific time period. While a balance sheet shows us a fixed point in time (remember the 'as of' found at the top of the page), the income statement represents a period of time such as a month, a quarter, or a fiscal year. In the same way that you and I have earnings and expenses each month, an income statement will tell you how much money a company made and spent during a certain period of time. In terms of Golden Flake's income statement, you can see that it is for the 52-week period ending 5/30/2008.

The purpose of the income statement is to show how much revenue a company earned and the costs associated with earning that revenue. The income statement is also the home of the notorious 'bottom line' of Wall Street and Fortune 500 lore. This is in fact a literal bottom line on the page, and it shows a company's net earnings or losses. The bottom line shows us the result after all revenues and expenses have been accounted for.

One metaphor commonly used with the income statement is that of a staircase – you start at the top with revenue, and then step-by-step deduct expenses until you get to the bottom, and the bottom line. The idea of this statement is to show how revenue is reduced to net income, and this makes the income statement somewhat easier to understand than the balance sheet. With the income statement you can just move down the page, or staircase, subtracting or adding as you go until you arrive at net income.

One of the most important things to understand about an income statement is that it does not show the inflow or outflow of cash. The income statement shows revenues and expenses – it does *not* show cash receipts (money received) or cash disbursements (cash paid.) According to accounting guidelines, revenue should be recognized when the seller has performed its obligation (delivered the product), and the buyer has agreed to purchase the product, and agreed to a price. This does not mean that the buyer has made the payment and cash has changed hands. As such, the income statement shows recognized revenues and expenses, but not cash flows.

A Statement Divided

The income statement is typically divided into two parts, the operating section and the non-operating section. For investors and lenders this division makes sense – they need to know what expenses and revenues are a direct result of regular business activities (the operating section), and which are not (the non-operating section). With a company such as Golden Flake, the operating section involves all of the revenues and expenses associated with making snack foods. In the non-operating section, a company will report any revenue or expense not directly associated with its regular operations, such as the sale of investments or a gain on the sale of assets.

The Real Deal

Now let's walk through Golden Flake's income statement for the

52-week period ending 5/30/2008.

Revenue: At the top of the income statement, or the top of the stairs, you will always find revenue. Revenue is simply recognized sales, or the money received from the sale of the company's products or services. Usually you will find net revenues, meaning returns and allowances have already been subtracted. For the year ended 5/30/2008, you can see that Golden Flake recorded $113.38 million in revenues.

Cost of Revenue (aka Cost of Goods Sold): The Cost of Goods Sold (commonly called COGS) represents all the costs associated with creating a company's products. This can include the cost of raw materials, the cost of manufacturing the product, or shipping and handling costs. For Golden Flake, the cost of revenue represents all the costs that went into producing the various snack foods.

Gross Profit: Gross profit and the gross profit margin can sound complicated, but the idea is amazingly simple. To get gross profit, just subtract costs of goods sold from total revenues, or:

Revenue – Cost of Goods Sold

The gross profit margin (or gross margin) is just gross profit divided by revenues, or:

(Revenue – Cost of Goods Sold) / Revenue

For Golden Flake, you can see that their gross profit is $54.62 million, while the gross profit margin is .48, or 48%. These figures reveal how efficient a company is at managing the production process. Gross profit margin tells us if a company is managing labor, machines, and supplies efficiently. In order to interpret this figure you must compare it to other competitors in the same industry. It wouldn't make any sense to compare a manufacturing company with a service company, as service companies tend to have lower COGS and therefore a higher gross margin.

Selling, General, and Administrative Expenses (SG&A): As we continue down the staircase there are other operating expenses that need to be subtracted from gross profit. SG&A expenses are typically the largest component of other operating expenses, and while these expenses are outside the manufacturing function, they are still integral to a company's operations. Unlike COGS, these expenses are not directly associated with production. Rather, SG&A expenses are a result of normal business operations or day-to-day activities.

Selling expenses typically include sales commissions, salaries, or advertising expenses directly related to selling a product. General and administrative expenses can include rent, utilities, executive salaries, or insurance, among many other things. You can see that for the 52 weeks ended 5/30/2008, Golden Flake had $53.06 million in SG&A expenses. And since management did not record any other operating expenses such as R&D or depreciation, total operating expenses equals COGS + SG&A. After the operating expenses are subtracted we arrive at, you guessed it, operating profit.

Operating Income (aka Operating Profit): Operating profit is just what it sounds like - it is the profit from a company's core business operations. When calculating operating profit you must take into account the expenses associated with directly producing a product (COGS) as well as any other operating expenses (SG&A, R&D, depreciation, etc).

Note: Sometimes, as is the case with Golden Flake, COGS are incorporated into total operating expenses. Other times, COGS will be a separate category, and operating expenses will be its own line item. In either case, operating profit will always be the amount earned after subtracting COGS and all other operating expenses.

EBIT and EBITDA: Operating profit is also sometimes called EBIT, or 'earnings before interest and taxes'. In short, EBIT reveals a company's ability to produce a profit before considering the costs of financing or taxes. Another fun metric is EBITDA, which takes EBIT one-step further and represents 'earnings before interest, taxes, depreciation and amortization'. EBITDA also eliminates the effects of accounting and financing decisions, and so it can be a good measure of operational profitability. But while EBITDA can be useful, this is a non-GAAP (Generally Accepted Accounting Principles) measure, so there is no legal requirement for companies to disclose EBITDA.

Next we can take the stairs down to the **non-operating section**. As discussed earlier, non-operating activities are income or expenses not associated with a company's core operations. Typical examples include interest expense, income from invest- ments, or a gain from the disposal of assets. As you can see, Golden Flake did not report any interest expense, but they did report a small gain on the sale of an asset, and some additional income categorized as "other".

Income Before Taxes: Once all non-operating activities are accounted for you have income before taxes, and since taxes rarely need their own explanation, the next step down is income after tax. For many companies, income after tax will be net income; however, Golden Flake allows for **minority interest** and **extraordinary items**. Minority interest represents the share of profit belonging to minority shareholders, while an extraor- dinary item is an unexpected one-time event. But since Golden Flake does not report any minority interests or extraordinary items for the 52 weeks ended 5/30/2008, net income stands at $1.13 million.

Net Income: And there you have it, the bottom line! Another phrase you hear bandied about in terms of the income statement is 'in the black', or conversely, 'in the red'. When a company is said to be 'in the black' it means that they have positive net income, but if a company is 'in the red' it means they are losing money, and are experiencing a net loss. The phrases came about simply due to ink color – when a company reports positive earnings they use black ink, while it has become industry standard to use red ink to show a negative number, or loss. Suffice to say, you want companies to be in the black, as Golden Flake is here.

Earnings per Share (EPS): This is another one of those terms that sounds complicated and grim, but earnings per share only represents the amount of profit that is allocated to each outstanding share. EPS tells us how much each share of stock would get if the company distributed all of its net income for the period in question. While there are several different methods that can be used to calculate EPS, common ways include:

(Net Income – Preferred Dividends) / Weighted Average Common Shares Outstanding

Or:

Net Income / Weighted Average Common Shares Outstanding

A weighted average is used to take into account the fact that the number of common shares outstanding can change during a period. Companies typically report basic EPS and diluted EPS, and you can see that Golden Flake has allocated a space for both. Diluted EPS takes into account what would happen if all potential shares became outstanding.

Conclusion

As with the balance sheet, these figures become more meaningful if you can compare a company to other companies in the same industry. Gross margin, operating profit, and net income vary widely across industries, so look at industry averages to see what is appropriate. The income statement is a valuable tool and reveals a company's profitability. When taken in conjunction with the other statements it is a good indicator of a company's ability to survive and prosper.

In Millions of USD (except for per share items)	52 weeks ending 2008-05-30	52 weeks ending 2007-06-01	52 weeks ending 2006-06-02	52 weeks ending 2005-06-03
Revenue	113.38	110.83	106.55	103.14
Other Revenue, Total	–	–	–	–
Total Revenue	**113.38**	**110.83**	**106.55**	**103.14**
Cost of Revenue, Total	58.77	57.98	57.02	55.40
Gross Profit	**54.62**	**52.85**	**49.53**	**47.74**
Selling/General/Admin Expenses, Total	53.06	51.48	49.17	48.02
Research & Development	–	–	–	–
Depreciation/Amortization	–	–	–	–
Interest Expense (Income) – Net Operating	–	–	–	–
Unusual Expense (Income)	–	–	–	–
Other Operating Expenses, Total	–	–	–	–
Total Operating Expense	**111.82**	**109.46**	**106.19**	**103.42**
Operating Income	**1.56**	**1.37**	**0.36**	**-0.28**
Interest Income (Expense), Net Non-Operating	–	–	–	–
Gain (Loss) on Sale of Assets	0.13	0.49	0.14	0.11
Other, Net	0.43	0.43	0.48	0.52
Income Before Tax	**1.90**	**2.02**	**0.69**	**0.10**
Income After Tax	**1.13**	**1.21**	**0.29**	**-0.01**
Minority Interest	–	–	–	–
Equity In Affiliates	–	–	–	–
Net Income Before Extra. Items	**1.13**	**1.21**	**0.29**	**-0.01**
Accounting Change	–	–	–	–
Discontinued Operations	–	–	–	–
Extraordinary Item	–	–	–	–
Net Income	**1.13**	**1.21**	**0.29**	**-0.01**
Preferred Dividends	–	–	–	–
Income Available to Common Excl. Extra Items	**1.13**	**1.21**	**0.29**	**-0.01**

The Income Statement

Income Available to Common

Including Extra Items	**1.13**	**1.21**	**0.29**	**-0.01**
Basic Weighted Average Shares	–	–	–	–
Basic EPS Excluding Extraordinary Items	–	–	–	–
Basic EPS Including Extraordinary Items	–	–	–	–
Dilution Adjustment	–	0.00	–	0.00
Diluted Weighted Average Shares	11.82	11.84	11.84	11.85
Diluted EPS Excluding Extraordinary Items	0.10	0.10	0.02	0.00
Diluted EPS Including Extraordinary Items	–	–	–	–
Dividends per Share – Common Stock				
Primary Issue	0.12	0.12	0.12	0.13
Gross Dividends – Common Stock	–	–	–	–
Net Income after Stock-Based Comp. Expense	–	–	–	–
Basic EPS after Stock-Based Comp. Expense	–	–	–	–
Diluted EPS after Stock-Based Comp. Expense	–	–	–	–
Depreciation, Supplemental	–	–	–	–
Total Special Items	–	–	–	–
Normalized Income Before Taxes	–	–	–	–
Effect of Special Items on Income Taxes	–	–	–	–
Income Taxes Ex. Impact of Special Items	–	–	–	–
Normalized Income After Taxes	–	–	–	–
Normalized Income Avail to Common	–	–	–	–
Basic Normalized EPS	–	–	–	–
Diluted Normalized EPS	0.09	0.08	0.02	-0.01

Chapter 18

The Statement of Cash Flows

Overview

Cash is essential. Without adequate cash, a company cannot pay employees, make debt payments, issue dividends, or acquire equipment. And if cash is essential, that means the statement of cash flows is essential too. This statement records the amount of cash that enters or leaves a company. It allows us to see where a company's money is coming from, and where it is being spent.

Also called the cash flow statement, this statement reports cash receipts, cash payments, and the overall net change in cash. The cash flow statement is divided into three separate categories – operating activities, investing activities, and financing activities. A company can be profitable according to accounting standards, but if it doesn't have enough cash to pay its obligations it will be in serious trouble. This is why analysts and investors pay such keen attention to the statement of cash flows.

Show me the Money!

As we discussed previously, the income statement does not represent cash inflows or outflows, as revenue and net income include sales made on credit. Think about your own personal cash flow – while you may be accustomed to making purchases on credit, at the end of the month you always need a handle on your actual cash flow, that is, your cash payments and cash receipts. Thus the statement of cash flows is different from the income statement and balance sheet in that does not include future incoming or outgoing cash that have been recorded on credit.

However, like the income statement, the statement of cash flows represents a period of time, specified in the heading. Here we will use the cash flow statement for the 26 weeks ending 11/28/2008.

Two Methods

There are two methods for presenting the statement of cash flows – the direct method and the indirect method. The difference in the two methods affects the presentation of the operating section only; the investing section and the financing section are presented the same way regardless of method. The key difference is that the direct method excludes depreciation, while the indirect method (as demonstrated by Golden Flake) starts with net income, adds back depreciation, and calculates changes in balance sheet items.

Cash from Operating Activities

As is common on all cash flow statements, with Golden Flake you can see that we begin with cash from operating activities. Total cash flow from operations is the most important line item on this statement – it shows how much cash is generated from day-to-day business operations.

We start with net income, and this is one way that the cash flow statement links to the other statements. The net income listed is taken directly from the income statement for that period. Here we have net income of $1.05 million.

The overall purpose of this section is to take the company's net income, and convert it to a cash basis. We do this by making adjustments for depreciation, gains and losses on the sale of assets, and by accounting for the changes in current assets and current liabilities.

Depreciation is a non-cash item that is often calculated into net income. Therefore, it needs to be reevaluated if you're calculating cash flow from operations. You can see that Golden Flake has made an adjustment for depreciation of $1.18 million, which is added to net income. Other adjustments include an adjustment for other non-cash items of ($0.85 million) and a change in working capital of ($0.28 million).

Change in Working Capital: Although this charge was minimal for Golden Flake, it is important to keep an eye on this figure if you're evaluating another company. A company's working capital is calculated as the excess of current assets over current liabilities, or:

Current Assets – Current Liabilities

The difference in working capital between two reporting periods is therefore the change in working capital. Current assets and current liabilities will increase or decrease throughout the year as a company funds its operations. If current assets increase it is a cash outflow: for example I paid for inventory and my cash balance went down. If current liabilities increase it is a cash inflow – for example I took on some short-term debt and received cash. By evaluating the change in working capital you can see the net effect of the changes in these asset categories during a certain period.

If the cash from operating activities is greater than net income this is generally a good sign. However, if cash from operating activities is less than net income, you need to examine why net income is not turning into cash.

Cash from Investing Activities

This section records any changes in the cash position that result from gains or losses in a company's investments. While investments may refer to investment positions in the financial markets or in subsidiaries, more often this category represents money earned or spent on a company's long-term assets. The change in cash position that results from acquisitions is also recorded in the investing section, so keep an eye for any cash outlays that a company has made to acquire another company.

Capital Expenditures: Unless a company made a large acquisition recently, the most important line item in this category is usually capital expenditures (or capex). Capital expenditures simply represent money spent to buy a fixed asset (growth capex) or to add value or extend the life of an existing asset (maintenance capex). If a company is showing a large figure for capex this may mean they are expanding, so it is important to keep an eye on any trends in this category.

Cash from Financing Activities

As the name would suggest, this section represents money that a company took in or paid out to finance its activities. In short, it shows the flow of cash between a company and its owners and creditors. Typical components of this section include the issuance or purchase of common stock, or the issuance or repayment of debt. Also included in this category is the payment of dividends, so always check the financing section to see what your company's dividend payment history is. For example, with Golden Flake you can see that $0.74 million was allocated towards the payment of dividends.

Unlike the operating section, negative cash flows from financing activities are not necessarily bad, as a negative cash flow from financing activities could indicate that a company has made a dividend payment or stock repurchase.

Conclusion

When you add the cash from operating, investing and financing activities you arrive at the net change in cash for a certain period. For Golden Flake, you can see that this sums to $2.0 million. This links the cash flow statement to the balance sheet, as the net change in cash is added to your existing cash account, to get your ending cash figure. Following the net change in cash you will often find supplemental information, including the cash paid for interest and taxes, as demonstrated on Golden Flake's statement.

I can't emphasize enough the importance of the cash flow statement. If a company is consistently generating cash it is good for stockholder value. This means a company will have cash to meet its obligations, but also may be able to increase or issue a dividend, buy back some of its stock, or reduce debt. In addition, there is little room to manipulate a company's cash flow, so oftentimes this statement will tell you the whole story. Many investors believe that 'cash is king', and indeed this is true to a certain extent, as positive, sustainable cash flow is essential for a firm's long-term success.

In Millions of USD (except for per share items)	26 weeks ending 2008-11-28	13 weeks ending 2008-08-29	52 weeks ending 2008-05-30	39 weeks ending 2008-02-29
Net Income/Starting Line	1.05	0.35	1.13	1.01
Depreciation/Depletion	1.18	0.58	2.29	1.72
Amortization	–	–	–	–
Deferred Taxes	–	–	-0.20	–
Non-Cash Items	-0.85	-0.04	-0.13	-0.08
Changes in Working Capital	-0.28	-0.05	0.35	-1.31
Cash from Operating Activities	**1.10**	**0.84**	**3.44**	**1.34**
Capital Expenditures	-0.67	-0.27	-2.30	-1.74
Other Investing Cash Flow Items, Total	2.69	0.05	0.19	0.12
Cash from Investing Activities	**2.02**	**-0.22**	**-2.11**	**-1.61**
Financing Cash Flow Items	-0.82	0.01	-0.57	-0.10
Total Cash Dividends Paid	-0.74	-0.37	-1.48	-1.11
Issuance (Retirement) of Stock, Net	-0.07	-0.02	-0.14	-0.11
Issuance (Retirement) of Debt, Net	0.51	-0.36	0.59	1.10
Cash from Financing Activities	**-1.12**	**-0.74**	**-1.59**	**-0.21**
Foreign Exchange Effects	–	–	–	–
Net Change in Cash	**2.00**	**-0.12**	**-0.26**	**-0.48**
Cash Interest Paid, Supplemental	0.11	0.06	0.22	0.15
Cash Taxes Paid, Supplemental	0.52	0.20	1.12	1.10

Lesson Six

Company Cultures – Or why Golden Flake

takes care of its employees

Chapter 19

Creating a Positive Company Culture

People will typically be more enthusiastic where they feel a sense of belonging and see themselves as part of a community than they will in a workplace in which each person is left to his own devices.
– Alfie Kohn

Introduction: As we reach the end of our Golden Flake journey, we enter the land, not of numbers and finances and accounting, but we enter the land of employees and the land of 'company culture', perhaps the most important part of any company.

Be nice to employees, they make the product

If your company does not make a profit, you do not have a job. The only way Golden Flake makes money is by selling a product. Sell a bag of chips and you have money coming in. Sell no chips and you have no money coming in. A very basic economic truth, but one that many people forget, e.g. the auto unions.

To ensure a profit, employees have to realize that 'we're all in this together'.

And Golden Flake works hard on developing that spirit of teamwork at Golden Flake.

I didn't make this up, but united we stand, separated we fall. The worse thing that can happen to a company is that it becomes divided into two camps. Employees versus Management.

And that leads us to a very basic economic principle – the problem of the commons, which has destroyed many companies. Again remember Detroit and the autoworkers.

The Problem of the Commons

Think about a pasture. Now anyone can keep their cows on this pasture. It is open to all. So if you raise cows, you want to keep as many cows as you can on this pasture. You want to take as much of the grass in the pasture to benefit yourself and your cows.

Because if you don't someone else will.

After all the pasture is open to everyone and it is pretty much every man for himself.

This arrangement might actually work pretty well, if it is a big pasture and there is plenty of grass to feed all the cows everyone starts keeping on the pasture.

But remember, one key lesson in economics is that resources are limited. And the grass in the pasture is limited. And there will come a day when there is just not grass to feed every cow. Especially if there has been no management, no regulator in place to allocate the grass.

Think buffalo here.

The buffalo herds in America were common. No one owned them. So each hunter tried to kill as many buffalo as he could to maximize the number of skins he could sell.

Unfortunately, because no one owned the buffalo, because there were no guidelines, regulating how many buffalo each person could kill, the buffalo almost became extinct.

Now back to our pasture.

Look, I am no dummy, I am going to feed as many cows as I can off of that pasture. I am going to take as much as I can, because if I don't the other guy will. In economics terms, I seek to maximize my gain.

Notice the key word here. I seek to maximize MY gain. I am in it for myself.

I have no sense of loyalty to my neighbors or their cows. I have no sense of community. I only know that I must grab as much of the pasture, as much of the grass as I can, so I can sell more cows.

In short, I am locked into a system that makes me think only of myself, and not think of the greater good of my neighbors. I want to increase my share of the pasture without limit, screw the other guy.

And now we can return to Detroit and the auto unions. The money that GM and other car companies were making was seen as a pasture. No one 'owned that money' in the eyes of the Union. It was like a common pasture, there for the taking. And if the union did not take as much of that money as it could, in benefits and pay raises, why heck, the other guy Mr. Management would take.

This theory of the commons, this theory of 'I better take as much out of the commons as I can', before the other guy does, destroyed Detroit.

And the unions kept taking more and more, until there was no grass left in the pasture.

If there had been some regulating force, say proper management of the pasture and a sense of 'we are all in this together', the pasture, in this case GM profits, wouldn't have been overgrazed.

But it was and now there is a much smaller pasture for American car companies. And unless a sense of community can be established between management and labor, the problem of the commons will start all over again.

Solving the Problems of the Commons

Quote: Life without a purpose is a languid, drifting thing; every day we ought to review our purpose, saying to ourselves, "This day let me make a sound beginning, for what we have hitherto done is naught!"
– *Thomas Kempis*

The Problem of the Commons can be simply stated: If there is no sense of obligation to a larger entity, be it a company, or a state, or a nation, why shouldn't every man be in it for himself.

As mentioned, the classic example was the buffalo herds. There was no one 'in charge' of the buffalo herds and every man shot as many buffalo as he could. After all, the more buffalo I shoot, the more money I make selling hides. There was no sense of obligation to preserve the buffalo, there was no greater purpose, the only objective was to make money.

Whoops, we almost bypassed an important word. Purpose. Buffalo hunting was merely a money-making game. With no sense of a higher purpose.

That brings us to the gist of what Golden Flake does so well.

If you want your company to succeed, you must establish a sense of loyalty and purpose in your employees. They must have a purpose they are working for.

On purpose

A sense of purpose? Let's say you are a tree chopper and the first day your boss tells you to go out and cut ten trees. You do that and the boss is so pleased that the next day he asks you to cut down 12 trees. You take your handy little ax, stroll out to the forest and chop down 12 trees. Well this continues, and at the end of the month, the boss has you chopping down 20 trees a day.

But you are dissatisfied, as you realize this could go on forever. The boss can keep raising the number of trees you chop down, until one day you lay down exhausted and just can't chop down any more trees. Heck, then he will replace you and get someone younger and stronger to chop down trees.

The boss has given you no purpose for chopping down trees. He didn't inspire you by saying how the trees you chopped down helped make homes for people or even a simple wooden deck where friends and family could gather. That would at least have given you a sense of purpose. A reason to keep cutting down trees.

And while the boss had you chop down trees, you were

feeling used. When you were worn-out, why wouldn't he cast you aside? He didn't show his loyalty by offering vacations, benefits, bonuses.

And the boss had violated a basic tenet of bossdom. Whenever two or more employees are gathered, tell them, and keep telling them the purpose of their work. The higher goal you, as a team, are all working for.

This all can be quickly encapsulated by the classic story of bricklayers.

A gentleman saw three men laying bricks.

He approached the first and asked, *"What are you doing?"*

Annoyed, the first man answered, *"What does it look like I'm doing? I'm laying bricks!"*

He walked over to the second bricklayer and asked the same question. The second man responded, *"Oh, I'm making a living."*

He asked the third bricklayer the same question, *"What are you doing?"* The third looked up, smiled and said, *"I'm building a cathedral."*

The third had a sense of purpose.

Okay, let's wrap this baby up. You always want to avoid 'The Problems of the Commons' in your company, where every employee, much like a buffalo hunter, is in it for themselves.

To imbue a sense of belonging and teamwork in employees, you must take their work out of the mundane world of hourly labor and imbue it with a sense of purpose. And you must communicate that sense of purpose to employees 'when and wherever two or more are gathered'.

The Real World of Golden Flake
A culture of working together

We had a culture at Golden Flake and we were protective of the culture to the extent that, yes you wanted outside ideas, but you didn't want somebody coming in and trying to revolutionize the culture. So I had two or three people I hired directly from Frito-Lay because we were the kind of company 'they used to be'.

They were a good company. Herman Lay ran a good company. People enjoyed working for him. And now it's taken them prisoner and some people do not want to work in that kind of environment. And I had a Frito-Lay man call me from Dallas one day and say, "Wayne, I know the kind of company you all are. We used to be that way and I have a man in manufacturing and he can't stand what they are asking him to do. Would you have a need for him?"

I said, "You tell him and his wife to come see me."

He and his wife came to Birmingham. I interviewed him. I found out that he was one of the Frito-Lay people who worked with them developing their corn chips, their Frito. I said I can use someone like that and we hired him and he became VP of Manufacturing.

That man and others from Frito-Lay came to us because of who we were.

I had the hardest time with one man we hired from Frito-Lay. He would say, "Well at Frito-Lay we did it this way."

And I had to say, "I never want to hear you say again, 'This is how we did it at Frito-Lay' We are not Frito-Lay and I don't want to hear it. Nobody else wants to hear it."

And I would stress that we were all in this together, again. You couldn't protect your turf. There was no 'my turf'. There was only 'our turf'. We all had different jobs and different titles. But we all had the same job of making this company successful. It doesn't matter whose turf it is, it doesn't matter who does it, it doesn't matter who gets the credit – we got to make it successful by doing it together.

I wouldn't let them have turfs and fights – that wasn't going to happen. So we ended up with good teamwork. That is the spirit we needed.

My day-to-day activities involve getting work done with

people. So my day-to-day activities were to ensure that everyone understood what needed to be done.

That is what leadership is. Being available to people. Being available to them, making sure they understand what our goal is, what we want to do, we all have a common interest in getting it done, then help them get it done. Give them the tools they need to accomplish the task we set out for them, give them some guidelines and let them use their own skills and individual talents and I tell them you can do everything it takes as long as it is legal, ethical and moral.

I would tell my people, "I don't want you to violate any of those things. We ran the company on biblical principles. The Golden Rule."

It is on our website too. They have polished it up a little bit now, about satisfying, making sure we have satisfied customers, employees. But it's all part of the same philosophy.

Plus, my door was never closed. Anybody could walk in. I would be in a visit with somebody, a meeting with somebody, and the door would be open and an employee would walk in and say, "I need to see you right now."

Okay.

I used to tell our people this. If you see somebody who looks like they have got a problem, go to them right now and ask if they have something they need to talk about. They have a problem, maybe we can fix it, maybe we can't. But I used to tell employees, "If you have a home problem, maybe we can't fix it, but we will listen." Because you don't need to go through life miserable and unhappy. You need to get up everyday and be excited about doing your job. If we can't figure out why, maybe you are in the wrong job. Cause you need to work and life is too short going through it being unhappy everyday.

– *Wayne Pate*

The importance of employee relations

Things happen. People may have problems that are not related to their work, but it affects their work. You are not going to find anything in a textbook about that. You are going to have a woman come into your office sobbing and crying and saying, "My 16 year old daughter has run away from home. What should I do?"

Well you don't read about that but those are the little things, but it's a big thing to her. Happy employees maintain good work habits. And when your 16 year old daughter runs away from home with a traveling salesman or something, you aren't very happy."

– *Wayne Pate*

Employee Relations

You must instill in employees a sense of belonging, a sense of the bigger picture – an employee can no longer come to work, do his job and go home, he has to have an overall knowledge of the 'bigger picture'.

Once a month in a meeting conducted by our COO, we have two plants, one in Birmingham and one in Florida, we have a meeting with everyone who was born in that month. Let's say you were born in the month of November, we go over how the company is doing and what is going on, how the financials are doing, what new products we have, what kind of challenges we have facing us.

Human Resource has a little thing, we talk about good manufacturing practices, any other little items that might come up during the month that we need to highlight and then of course we always answer questions.

Part of the financial part of the meeting is talking about the 401K. We are trying to keep people encouraged to stay the course right now in the tough economic times we're in.

Basically the most important part of the meeting is to get

people to ask questions at the end, to make it so you are not so high on your horse that a regular hourly employee can't ask a question. And they ask pointed questions, I always enjoy the question part.

Some groups you get a lot of good questions, some groups only one or two, but it is about keeping the employees in the loop, it is very important.

We do the same thing in Florida; it is a smaller operation. We don't do it on a birthday schedule, we do it in a rotating basis, because there might only be two or three employees at a meeting and I try to get at least six or eight involved in every meeting.

It keeps the line of communication open and we do the same thing with the sales side.

We had a meeting with the local sales regions yesterday, we go to Jackson, Mississippi next week; it is a lot of effort and time but the smaller group really keeps that communication alive. We started this concept in 1988; we call it the Birthday Meeting.

We started the meetings to increase employees' understanding of the company and to show that they have ownership. The meetings started out with "my chair is broken, I have this..." The little petty things they should be handling with their line supervisor every day.

But now the meetings cover bigger issues, like where are we moving in health care. Many employees are shocked if you have to increase the amount they pay for health care. Yet, here at Golden Flake, it was zero shock because we talked about it for 12 months with our employees.

We said to our employees, health care is moving up, here are the trends we see and what it is going to affect. When it came about, the employees were prepared for it, because we had been talking about it for 12 months.

And we realized that when we have a small meeting of

employees, we are not just talking to those employees in the room. If you talk to a group of four from the second shift, they are going to go out and talk about it to everyone else, so it has been a great concept.

Communicating and having meetings with employees takes a lot of time and Dave [Jones] does not always enjoy coming down here at 11 o'clock at night to speak with a group, but it is important for that communication and that is what it is all about, it's about communication.

Employees need to know they have an impact every day on what they do on their jobs and they need to know that we are concerned with their financial well-being from a personal standpoint too; we want to make sure they have benefits they can afford, provide them with decent health care.

A single employee on our health plan a week pays about $20 a week, and in the meetings we talk about the ratio, the employee pays 30%, we pay 70%.

In one meeting, I talked about an article I just read the other day, that nationally a single employee getting what the newspaper said was a decent health care plan pays about $60 a week. I have made sure to cover items like that. If you are an employee you might not do a lot of reading off the job; employees have to be motivated, they need to know what is going on outside of Golden Flake and health care is a big issue, so we talk about that.

We also talk with the employees about earnings per share and I go through that concept every time, what earning per share is.

Last year, we earned a dime per share and we have 11.8 million shares of stock. That comes out to a lot of dimes which comes out to 1.8 million dollars at the end of the year, so I give it to them like an analyst would talk about it but try to quantify it in a way that they can understand it, that 10 cents a share means 1.8 million dollars spread over 11.8 million shares.

We also post our financials on the website and they have access to that and every day the stock price is posted, right outside the HR department. The earnings press release is always posted right outside the employee entrance so they can see it; they might glance at it.

Employees need to know that by being productive and through other things, they can help influence our success. We know money talks and that's why we have bonuses that emphasize what they can do makes a difference in the future of our company. Bonuses also emphasize that you have ownership in things, and in sales we moved the bonuses right down to the route salesman.

In the plant we have an incentive bonus based on goals set for quality, for pounds produced per hour, for quality cases loaded on trucks per hour, so they have their goals – it is a plant-wide thing – it is also peer pressure – Jon, you are not doing your job and you are hurting my bonus.

We found that peer pressure works better than management. That applies to most situations in the plant, including safety. If you have too many accidents, no safety bonus.

And the bonus programs apply to everyone. You might say, "Okay, I am the custodian, what do I do, I'm just the custodian?" Well, custodians understand what they do is important and we must get superiors on all our inspections.

Without superiors on inspections, we would lose our private label and government contracts.

And a sales route person understands that the more he sells, the more he makes, his bonus is attached to hitting certain goals and things.

– *Mark McCutcheon*

Golden Flake's Mission

We believe in a mission, not a mission statement; mission statements are things lawyers come up with and no one pays attention to them. Our mission is satisfying the expectations of our consumer, the person who eats our products, our customers, the people that allow us to sell our product in their establishments, without them we have no place to sell, no Golden Flake at all.

Our mission also includes satisfying the expectation of each of our employees, who we hope is a consumer and is a stockholder. Our employees are the second biggest shareholders of Golden Flake.

And of course we want to satisfy the expectations of our outside stockholder. It is our goal to satisfy the expectations of our core group, consumers, customers, employees and stockholders, and that is a real balancing act in doing that.

We are about selling fun and that's what makes this company so fun to work for, rather than working for the other industries in town: steel, health care, pipe, real estate.

Our stuff is all about fun; that is what we do – sell fun.

– *Mark McCutcheon*

Communication is the key

Communication is the key to everything; we have health fairs, pedometers. Our CFO is wearing one right now for a walking promotion. There are many steps you can take through an educational program to make employees more proactive in taking care of their health which saves dollars.

The closer you are to your group of employees the better you can keep that open communication; friends of ours in the industry used to be a lot like us. They are a little larger than us, but they have drifted away from their employees. They have added a bunch of VPs, they put some layers in and they don't want to be on the plant proper. They have gone and rented space in an office building because they think that builds better public perception.

All it does is distance you from your employees. And you never want that.

There is another company from the Northeast that has headquarters in Atlanta which is really stupid just because the former president was from Georgia and that is where he wanted to be.

Unfortunately some executives are detached and some feel the need to be detached.

Heck, we once had a Golden Flake executive dining room. It used to be an old barbecue place down the street and it closed.

The more you are around folks, the better the communication. The more you isolate yourself, you are no longer in the employees' world. You are in your world and you are not understanding the custodian's world or the packer's world or the route salesman's world.

We try to get out, I went out twice last week, rather than visiting stores, visiting customers trying to come across route people, just trying to see what is going on, what is going on in their lives, what they are seeing – good, bad, indifferent – because you are now one on one with them; you show that you care and they appreciate it.

– *Mark McCutcheon*

Lesson Seven
How to succeed in business

Chapter 20

How To Get Promoted

Success in business requires training and discipline and hard work. But if you're not frightened by these things, the opportunities are just as great today as they ever were.

– David Rockefeller

Introduction: A recurring theme in this book is that you can never know too much. The Maillard effect, the impact of legislation and lobbyists on your business, the impact of regulations on the packaging labels, how to maximize the use of your raw materials, how to run a transportation business, how to operate a sewer system. Time and time again, this book has shown how these factors can come into play forcing businessmen to be multi-dimensional thinkers.

That's why every top executive at Golden Flake worked their way through the system, starting at the bottom, on the production line or running a route to learn the complicated real world we all live in, even when you're just 'making chips'.

How to succeed

What does it take to make it in business? A desire to work hard. A willingness to move. A willingness to learn. Taking on projects that make you stand out, that show your talent. A strong education in every aspect of the business, knowing every aspect of the business, not just your small sector of the business. Working your way up through levels of the business and learning every step of the way what really makes the business work.

Realizing that you do not have a nine-to-five job, you have a passion and really enjoy what you do. Setting goals for yourself. Setting time limits for yourself. Where do you want to be in five years? What will it take to get there? What kind of sacrifices? What do you have to learn? Are you willing to do that? And again, being appreciated as a hard worker who gets the job done, who is willing to take risks, take on projects that might be new.

And that is why this section is important. It shows what takes to succeed to become a vice president, president, CEO.

The lessons are explained by Wayne Pate, Director of Golden Flake, who has over 40 years experience with Golden Flake and who has held numerous positions including President of Golden Flake. And he has seen employees come and go and knows what it takes to make it 'to the top'.

Note that Mr. Pate's career did not just happen by accident. He knew what he wanted and made sure he was prepared to take advantage of opportunities as they arose.

The making of a CEO
Have a goal and train yourself well

I grew up on a farm in south Georgia. Loved farming, always wanted to be a farmer. I wanted to go to college, I was very involved in FHA – those were the things that the University of Georgia would have. When I got ready to go to college, somehow or the other, I didn't want to go to the University of Georgia. I wanted to go to the best school in the state which was Georgia Tech.

I almost went to Auburn, but I didn't do that. I went to Georgia Tech, even though they don't teach agriculture, with the intent of being a farmer. And my goal was that I would go to Tech, study industrial management, which gave me a lot of business background – industrial management, corporate finance accounting, and cost accounting – and a lot of math, algebra, trig, analytic math, statistics, calculus – all of those.

I wanted to study industrial management with civil engineering which would give me soils and geology and all those things. The other part of my plan was, okay I am going to work for industry for five years and the reason for five was I needed to get business experience because I don't need to go work for somebody and not ever be able to make a contribution.

I feel that in five years, I will be able to make a contribution. I will be trained by Georgia Tech, business experience and I will go back to south Georgia and start farming. I figured my daddy could teach me everything I needed to know about farming.

But I got to Texaco and got promoted rapidly. Boom, boom, boom. I chose that industry because I did a report in statistics on the oil business at Tech. Got interested in the oil business and looking around there was Standard, Gulf, Shell and Texaco.

I went to work for Texaco and they moved me five times in six years. I got promoted every time. I was hired with 28 other people and I got promoted faster than any of the others. Boom, boom, boom.

I met my wife. We got married. I forgot about the five-year plan. And I ended up in Birmingham and they were fixing to move me again to Hawaii, Florida or Mississippi. And I had moved, as I said, five times in six years and I wanted to start a family and I kind of wanted to settle down. And I knew with Texaco that eventually I end up in New York and I didn't want that. I was being promoted pretty rapidly and that was where headquarters was and I could just see it coming. That was good – I was being promoted, but I didn't really want to move to New York.

So I started to look around and I went to an industrial psychologist who had a lot of contacts with companies and he told me about Golden Flake, and I went over there expecting to spend half an hour and I spent half a day with Mr. Townes visiting. I did not meet Mr. B (Mr. Bashinsky, owner) at that time as Mr. Townes was the executive officer and he told me all the needs they had and he said I want you to come back and meet some others.

So I went back and spent another long period of time. I remember talking to Mr. B and he said, "What is it going to take for you to come to work for us. We can't pay you what you need – what you want. We can't pay you that much, but we sure do need you to come."

I said okay and about then I really wanted to go over there. I said, "Well can I be making this much money in five years if I do the job for you?" And he said, "Without a doubt."

"Okay," I said. "I know you don't give company cars to employees, but I have always had one and I want a company car."

"Okay!"

Get to know the business in EVERY aspect

So I went to work. I did not know what my job was. They gave me all kinds of stuff to start with. The first thing they did was say the basis of our business is route sales so we want you to go ride on a route truck for two weeks.

And that was my first job at Golden Flake, riding on a route truck. They told me, "So when the salesman comes in today, just go on the route with him."

That is how I met Fred Gyger. We remained friends until that man died. Anyway I met him about 4:30 a.m. and we worked on that route. Well, he went on vacation and so his supervisor ran his route. That was the way it was, when a man went on vacation, his supervisor would run the route for him.

So the second week, I was always good with numbers, so the supervisor wanted me to keep the accounts on the route. We did a lot of cash business and so I kept up with the money. Collected the bills, wrote the tickets, did all of that. I could balance it to the penny. Most of them couldn't.

He was so fascinated that he went and told Mr. Townes that I was the best man he ever had that could run a route.

Well I enjoyed that, and then I came back in and Mr. Townes said, "Now I want you to go into the plant and I want you to write operating procedures for all the factory work."

I went into the plant and chatted with every cook, and learned all about operating temperatures and all the fine points about cooking potato chips.

Let me back up here a moment; when I went to work for Golden Flake, they had made it a public company. They were smart enough to start hiring college graduates to be managers to run the business. The first crop had been there eight years when I got there.

Anyway, after I spent about three months of learning how chips were made, they called a meeting.

They called in the head of manufacturing, the head of sales, all the managers and said, "We have made some decisions."

They had been trying to buy a company in Atlanta that made pork skins under federal inspection and made cheese curls and puff curls and corn chips and tortilla chips. They wanted to buy the company so Golden Flake would be able to produce those things. At that point we were buying them from someone else.

They said, "The people in Atlanta want too much for the business. We won't be able to buy it. Therefore we are going to make our own pork skins, our own cheese curls, our own corn chips, our own tortilla chips."

Mr. B looked at me and said, "Wayne, I want you to honcho it."

I did not know one thing about a corn chip or a tortilla chip or a pork skin.

He said, "I want you to head it up."

So I said, "All right, and point me in one direction where I can start finding out something."

Mr. Townes said, "Go to Atlanta and visit with…"

He gave me two names, and one of the guys was running the factory we had tried to buy and couldn't, and we were still buying products from them. But I couldn't believe how nice he was to me. He knew that we were going to stop buying from them and start our own factory, but he was still a great help.

I started traveling all over the country visiting manufacturers. I went into everybody's plant except Frito-Lay's.

Anyway I knew that I had to learn, if we were going to be able to do these things I had to learn.

I also knew that we had to learn how to make pork skins under federal inspection. I went to Atlanta and sat down with the FDA regional office.

I said, "All right, we are going to build us a pork skin plant. You tell us what you want."

I designed that pork skin plant. I designed every square inch of that plant where every drain, every fountain, where everything in that place was. I laid it out. But I kept in constant communication with the FDA. The time came, this was my first real big project, the time came and I made an appointment with the FDA in Washington. The company had tried this before. They had mailed stuff up there before and it took weeks and nothing ever happened and then they turned us down.

Well, I took a different approach. I believe in involving people, so I made the appointment in Washington and I also called my USDA people in Atlanta. I said, "Before I go to Washington, I am going to bring the plans by and I want your opinion and approval before I go."

I went to see him and he said, "Wayne, you won't have any trouble with these plans."

Got on a plane, went to Washington, had an appointment the next morning and the guy walks in and looks at the plans and says, "Well, I don't see but one thing that I would like changed. I need to see you make these foot-operated lavatories instead of hand-operated lavatories."

I said, "Done."

He said, "Approved."

I got my plans, came back to Birmingham and started to buy everything we needed for a pork skin plant. Having purchased that I stated revamping the whole plant, knocking out walls...

The interesting thing was that two or three of us were traveling together to visit each plant; we really learned a lot just by asking questions and I was always observing when I was asking. Because sometimes people would tell you they were doing one thing and they weren't.

The fact is that a lot of people don't have a procedure. They think they are following a procedure but they are not. So we learned that if you do this, you get this. If you do this, you get this. We came back and set up a formula, a process, for how we were going to make corn chips.

I had to buy the equipment. No questions asked, I spent 28 million in a very short period of time, I tell you. The first corn chip we made, the cookers were huge. I bought a cooker that made 750 pounds of corn chips an hour. In less than a year we were close to selling more corn chips than we could make.

When we first started making corn chips, I kept testing and testing. I went outside and tested hem. And we got public opinion on flavor and when four out of five people preferred our corn chip to Frito, I said I believe we have it.

And soon instead of our 750-pound cooker, we had to get a 2,000-pound cooker. And then we added tortilla chips. I think that Golden Flake is making a better tortilla chip than anybody in the world.

We were successful with the corn chips. Then we took potato storage and made a cheese operation out of it. I also did the same type of research on cheese curls, cheese puffs. I visited all the factories, saw what they did, so I am not reading in a book what it is all about. I knew what it was all about. Quality manufacturers, stood behind their product, good reputation, they knew what they doing – there wasn't a chance they just worked it out.

Now we have always bought our equipment from the same manufacturer, who was a friend of Mr. B. But we bought from a different manufacturer to build the corn puff manufacturing area. Now it comes time to replace the potato chip cooker.

Mr. B, who was the primary owner of the business, as I said, had developed a friendship with a certain manufacturer. He let me do all the other stuff, buy the equipment for making corn chips, cheese puffs, but now it was time to replace the potato chip fryer.

So my buddies and I planned to do the same thing. Carefully look at all the cookers and buy the best one available. So I said to Mr. B, "Do you want to go with us. We're getting ready to go look at some potato chip fryers."

And he said, "You boys go make the decision."

So we did our research. One of the things I did was make a little block of colored wood and I could time how long it took to go through the system, and we did that with every fryer we looked at. Anyway – after visiting and visiting, we decided that a certain manufacturer had the best system. The best engineered, the best cooker. The total dwell time, the time the chip spends in the oil, and the temperature, better than anybody.

Well Mr. B was kind of disappointed.

I remember the day we told him that we were not going with his friend's cooker; he said, "Well, let's order it."

Then he said, "Before we order it, let's sit down and do some planning. Let's delay buying that cooker a little bit. Wayne, do you think you can set us up some more trips to visit cookers..."

I said, "Sure, I can do that."

So we didn't buy a cooker. I set up some more visits. You would have thought we had done everything wrong. Mr. B pointed out every good thing about what he wanted to buy and he was just anti what we wanted to buy. But the more we looked, the more convinced I was that we had made the right decision.

Then the day came after we had made several more visits, Mr. B said, "Wayne, call my friend to fly down to Birmingham."

And I'm thinking, "Uh oh, he's going to tell him he is going to buy a cooker from him."

Well Mr. B comes into my office and his friend comes into my office and I didn't know this was going to happen. I didn't know what was going on. Then Mr. B started chewing out his friend and his friend's staff.

You have never heard a chewing out that those men got, that he gave them.

He said, "You all have sat on your butts and you have let the competition do this better and this better and this better. You all..."

And he went on and on and ripped them up and down and not only didn't give them an order, but said we are buying from the competition.

And after that Mr. B wrote us a note, the three of us who had been involved, and he said, "I want you all to know that you were right and I was wrong. I am a thousand percent behind you."

He never really questioned us again.

I went on and built the Florida plant and then remodeled the Nashville plant. We had the best manufacturing then and now. I tell you – no one can manufacture better or more efficiently than Golden Flake. I have been to plants all over this country and nobody does it better than us.

You must have a management philosophy and stick with it

After doing all the things in manufacturing, Mr. B says, "Okay, now we have to get our sales organization in shape."

I was Head of Manufacturing and Human Resources and Risk Management. After we got manufacturing in top-notch shape, I was lucky enough to take over sales. I had expressed some ideas of what I thought we should do in sales.

So I wrote a letter to the sales representatives and said these are the things that we want to accomplish. I started listing the things that I think we needed to do. And they thought it was the clear direction they wanted. Some of them had the clear directions framed and put on their walls.

The point is, I was trying to focus on the things that we needed to do to accomplish what we wanted to accomplish. They really got behind it and I remember saying if we can do this, it will save us 3.8 million dollars in costs. And I listed the reasons why we needed to do things – they worked hard.

I had all the sales managers report directly to me. I had seven. I found out that I had too many. I started cutting, reorganizing all of that. Anyway, I don't remember when I became President. I can't remember what happened.

Tom Davis had always helped me run things and he said, "I want to retire." I said, "Tom, please don't leave me now. I don't have a vice president of sales. At least stay until I get a vice president of sales."

He said okay and didn't say another word.

How you find good people

After I became President, I needed a Sales VP, and I started interviewing around for a VP and I asked each sales manager how they would run the sales organization and it was interesting the answers I got. I asked them if they would be interested in being VP, what they thought about it, what they thought the job was and I got down to the youngest one in the bunch, Randy Bates, and he said, "Do I have an opportunity to do that job?" And I said, "You sure do."

And he said, "You just tell me what I need to learn and what I need to do. I want that job."

I said, "Okay."

And I laid it out for him, what he needed to learn and what he needed to do. So after some months went by, I called him and said I just moved the sales manager out of Florida because I needed him in Birmingham. That was Jim Ward. Jim has been a blessing. I mean I love the guy, he came and helped me in a time I really needed help. He was excellent with computers and very analytical. He is the best salesman I have ever known.

He can build relationships and that's what is so important. Relationships are critical in anything you do.

Anyway, I called Randy Bates down in New Orleans and I said, "Randy, I need you to move to Florida and take over Florida."

All he said was, "When do you want us there?"

He went to Florida and did a great job. I called him one day and said, "Randy, I need you in Atlanta. You have to take over Georgia."

So finally one day I called him up. This is not snap, snap. This is over time. I called him up and said, "Randy, you know that job you've been wanting. I need you in Birmingham today."

One day he walked into my office and handed me a piece of paper. He had written a goal for himself to be Sales Vice President of Golden Flake by a certain date. He had beaten that date by about a year and a half.

But he had a plan. And he was willing to do the things he needed to do to prepare him for the job. And as it turned out, Randy started on a route right here in Birmingham. He worked Nashville, New Orleans, Orlando and Atlanta. He covered the whole company. He knew every salesperson we had and he knew every customer we had – all the stores, everything. He knew the territory.

Mark, our current President, didn't want to come to work for us. He said, "Why would I go to Auburn and then drive a potato chip truck?"

His daddy encouraged him. So Mark came to Golden Flake and we put Mark in corn chips. Mark worked, now here is an Auburn graduate, Mark worked third shift, which is the hottest, most undesirable job you imagine. He never complained. But he was a standout as he worked hard.

So one day I called Mark and said, "Mark, I want you and

Terri to move to Ocala. We're getting ready to open the new plant and I want you to go down there and get a culture established like we got here. You and Terri can get us established in the community and..."

And he said, "I don't want to..."

He was living in an apartment at his grandmother's house and had no real expenses.

I said, "Look, let me tell you something, we may never ever be able to offer you an opportunity like this again."

About thirty minutes, his daddy called, "You're moving my youngest?"

"Yes sir, that's where they need to be."

Mark moved down there. He did everything better than what I could have imagined. In the community. With the sales organization. He set that thing up and ran that thing and it has always been great. Had a great system.

During that time, when he was down there, they had a little girl, who gave them their first grandbaby last week. Mark's daughter used to ride in my lap in the company plane. I used to bring her back to her grandparents in Birmingham.

Mark did a super job. He started there really learning a lot about the sales organization. So one day I called him and said, "Mark, you have to come back to Birmingham."

And he said, "I don't want to come back to Birmingham. We like it here."

About 15 minutes later his daddy calls and says, "Thank you for bring my youngest back home."

So anyway, Mark came back and he did everything here that we asked him to do and when it became closer to the time I was going to retire, I said, "Do you want to become President?"

Mark has done a terrific job. He's a super – I call him 'young man' but he is over 50 now – not a young man.

– *Wayne Pate*

Paying your dues

I have been 30 years with the company. I was in route sales training. I didn't know if I was going to get a route, they hired me in as an extra person in downtown Birmingham; they hired me in without even having a route to go. I went from running a hot dog stand route to pretty much holding every position in the sales department you can hold as I worked my way up the ranks.

— *Randy Bates*

Learn the business

What do I do in a day? Yesterday we talked about cost increases in one of our lines; we made adjustments in weight and price we needed to make going forward, so we made our decisions... I dealt with a charity board, then went to a sales meeting, meeting and greeting with them. I also stopped in on a spice meeting.

I manage by walking around. The only thing I failed to do yesterday, I was going to go out on the line and I didn't make that.

What else did I do? Employee issues and someone died and we talked with a new pork skin provider and wrote a note to a stockholder that had a stroke.

We all wear a lot of hats around here, a company this size, there are not a lot of levels here; if you work for Alabama Power there are a lot of levels.

We tell our folks there are not a lot of little levels here; you just need to learn anything you can anywhere you can. We try to challenge people in certain areas, so they can get the broad scope of what is going on.

When I started here, in just six months I was on second shift in production and then third shift and my wife didn't really care for that, but that was where I needed to go to learn.

That is how I learned the business, my bosses said this is

what you need to do to learn the business and that is what we try to do, provide the opportunity for those people to learn so we can find the area that they are best in.

– *Mark McCutcheon*

Chapter 21

The Players

Mr. Randy Bates is Executive Vice President of Sales, Marketing and Transportation for Golden Flake. He has held these positions since October 26, 1998. Mr. Bates was Vice President of Sales from October 1, 1994 to 1998. Mr. Bates has been employed by Golden Flake since March 1979.

Mr. David Jones is Executive Vice President of Operations, Human Resources and Quality Control for Golden Flake. He has held these positions since May 20, 2002. Mr. Jones was Vice President of Manufacturing from 1998 to 2002 and Vice President of Operations from 2000 to 2002. Mr. Jones has been employed by Golden Flake since 1984.

Mr. Mark W. McCutcheon is President, Chief Executive Officer and Director of Golden Enterprises, Inc. and President of Golden Flake Snack Foods, Inc., a wholly owned subsidary of the Company. He was elected President and Chief Executive Officer of the Company on April 4, 2001 and President of Golden Flake on November 1, 1998. He has been employed by Golden Flake since 1980.

Mr. F. Wayne Pate is Director of Golden Enterprises, Inc. He retired as President of the Company on May 31, 2000. He served as President from November 1, 1998 until retirement. He also served as President of Golden Flake Snack Foods, Inc., a wholly-owned subsidiary of the Company from September 20, 1991, to November 1, 1998.

Ms. Patty Townsend is Chief Financial Officer, Vice President and Secretary of Golden Enterprises, Inc. She was elected Chief Financial Officer, Vice President and Secretary of the Company on March 1, 2004. She has been employed with the Company since 1988.

Julie McLaughlin is the marketing director for Golden Flake.

**BUSINESS
BOOKS**

Business Books encapsulates the freshest thinkers and the most
successful practitioners in the areas of marketing, management,
economics, finance and accounting, sustainable and ethical
business, heart business, people management, leadership,
motivation, biographies, business recovery and development
and personal/executive development.